Great Gardens

THE BEST OF
FINE GARDENING®

Great Gardens

The Taunton Press

Cover photo: Nancy Beaubaire

Back-cover illustration and photos:
left, Natalie Forsberg Siegel; center, Mark Kane;
right, Mary Carolyn Pindar

Taunton
BOOKS & VIDEOS
for fellow enthusiasts

First printing: March 1994
Printed in the United States of America

A FINE GARDENING Book

FINE GARDENING® is a trademark of The Taunton Press, Inc.,
registered in the U.S. Patent and Trademark Office.

The Taunton Press
63 South Main Street
Box 5506
Newtown, CT 06470-5506

Library of Congress Cataloging-in-Publication Data

Great gardens.
     p. cm. — (The Best of fine gardening)
    Articles originally published in Fine gardening magazine.
    "A Fine gardening book"—T.p. verso.
    Includes index.
    ISBN 1-56158-078-3
    1. Gardens — United States. 2. Gardens — United States —
Pictorial works. 3. Gardens — Design. I. Fine gardening.
II. Series.
SB466.U6G69 1994   93-41877
712'.6 — dc20   CIP

Contents

Introduction

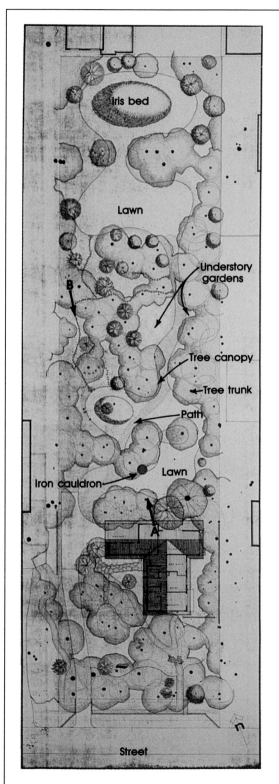

Iris bed

Lawn

Understory gardens

Tree canopy

Tree trunk

Path

Iron cauldron

Lawn

B

A

N

Street

Here are the best of the gardens profiled by *Fine Gardening* magazine in its first five years of publication.

In this beautifully illustrated collection, skilled gardeners throughout the United States open their gardens to you, sharing how they transformed their visions of idyllic landscapes into satisfying realities. From entryways to backyards, whole properties to intimate patios, sunny flower borders to shady groves, these gardens offer imaginative solutions to the most common challenges all gardeners face. Among the gardens profiled, you're sure to find ideas that you can adapt to your property, whether your garden is young or mature.

You'll find the articles in this collection especially helpful and inspiring because they are the work of enthusiasts, gardeners who have spent years developing their properties and want to help you enjoy your garden too. Sharing their hard-won experience, the authors tell you the problems they faced, what they wanted from their gardens and how they combined existing features with new plants and structures to achieve their goals.

The editors of *Fine Gardening* hope you'll experiment with the ideas in this collection of articles. No matter which you choose to try, your efforts will be rewarded.

"The Best of *Fine Gardening*" series collects articles from back issues of *Fine Gardening* magazine. A note on p. 96 gives the date of first publication for each article; product availability, suppliers' addresses and prices may have changed since then. Other books in the series include *Perennials, Shrubs & Trees* and *Garden Design Ideas*.

In 40-odd years of gardening and building, the author and his wife have transformed a property that started as a vacant lot. In the photo above, three large projects are on view: the pond at left, the formal gardens and sitting area in the foreground, and the ornamental plantings on the slope in the background. (Taken at A on site plan, p. 11.)

A Lifelong Garden

The fruit of 40 years of care and love

by F. Reed Estabrook, Jr.

My wife, Nancy, and I are both avid gardeners, but I'm the mechanic—I enjoy big jobs—and Nancy is the horticulturist. Between us, over the past 44 years we've transformed a vacant lot into the beautiful property you see in the photo on the facing page. We've learned on our feet, and when we finish one project we start another. As Nancy says, "That's gardening."

We bought our lot in a town near Boston in 1946. We had two young children and we planned to build a house. The property was a 1½-acre triangle, with the longest side fronting a road. The land ran flat for 120 ft. back from the road, then dived down a steep slope and leveled out briefly 40 ft. below before dropping again to a broad marsh on the Charles River. With the lot, we got a tired stone wall, a lot of weeds, some nice old trees, and a basement that had once supported a house.

If you visited us today, you'd see a front yard planted to beds of pachysandra, perennial borders, foundation trees and shrubs, and a large much-groomed lawn. From the backyard you'd look down on a slope completely planted in ornamental trees, shrubs and perennials, with a grass path switching back and forth across the slope and leading to a pond, gravel paths and formal gardens at the foot of the slope (see site plan, p. 11). You'd also see a house, a garage with a barn loft, and a fenced work area with bins for storing compost, sand, gravel and shredded leaves. Aside from the house and a few old trees, everything is our handiwork. We hired contractors on a few occasions, mainly for heavy backhoe and bulldozer jobs, but otherwise we did the building and gardening ourselves, with help from friends and our children.

I'm an engineer, and I enjoy moving stones, excavating, shredding leaves, and making tools and machinery that let me tackle these jobs single-handed. I also do the lawn, prune the hedges, and rake the gravel driveway and paths. Nancy has

shoveled and wheelbarrowed many cubic yards of dirt, but her real love is plants. She chooses them, keeps a good-size collection growing in nursery beds before transplanting them, and is constantly changing the garden's look, pulling plants when she finds something she likes better.

Lawn

Early on, we set out to make a beautiful lawn in the front yard. We needed topsoil, and luckily we found 10 in. to 12 in. of rock-free loam at the bottom of our property. To get the loam up the slope, I built a sort of funicular railway, with 2x4 tracks, and a car with pipe axles, wooden wheels with sheet-metal flanges and an old wheelbarrow body for a hopper. We tied a pulley to a tree limb, ran a rope around it and hauled loads up the slope, taking power at one time or another from our car, a hand windlass and a small gasoline engine with a gear box. We dug and hauled enough loam to spread 4 in. over all the ground in front and to one side of the house, an area roughly 70 ft. by 125 ft. The job took all summer. By my calculations, we moved 108 cu. yd. of loam, at least eight dumptrucks' worth. The digging, hauling, screening, leveling, seeding, rolling and hand-watering burn in my memory.

A good lawn is hard to make. In the early years, we pursued weeds relentlessly. (Nancy would sometimes send the children to pick bouquets of dandelion flowers from our neighbors' lawns to keep the seeds from blowing to our lawn.) Heat waves during vacations ruined our lawn several times—we came home to patches of dead brown grass. We've since installed an automatic watering system. I mow at least 2 in. high through the summer to keep the grass strong, and then gradually lower the cut in the fall. By leaf fall, the turf is short and I can blow leaves off easily. Every Labor Day weekend we pull crabgrass, reseed bare patches, and sod the weak spots along the driveway if seeds refuse to take. Each year we find we have less work and a stronger lawn.

Gardens

We were beginners when we started to garden. Nancy likes to say that she didn't

know a rose from a petunia. In the early 1950s, just after we had finished the house and moved in, a man knocked on the door. He said that a lady down the street had died recently and he had an order of plants for her that he would sell us very reasonably. Nancy had to use the dictionary to find forsythia, winged euonymus and barberry, and thought they sounded lovely. We had no idea that these plants are not only common but also a snap to root from cuttings. When the package arrived, we found rooted sticks. We planted them, but they took years to amount to anything, and as we grew more knowledgeable and our tastes changed, we replaced most of them with more interesting plants.

We designed the landscape as we went along. Our front yard is fairly conventional, with expanses of pachysandra under the oldest trees, a perennial border along the rock wall, shrubs and small trees and flower beds framing the house, and the much-groomed lawn.

The slope behind the house, on the other hand, has been a challenge to plant. We try to give it interest through the four seasons with perennials that bloom at different times, shrubs and trees for spring and fall color, and dwarf evergreens, and we grow ornamentals in masses so they look attractive both from afar and close up. Along one side of the pond, we've traded for land with our neighbor four times (his low land for our high land) and gradually added enough property to turn our triangle into a rectangle. We've made formal gardens on the new land. They start near the marsh with a curving row of azaleas, rhododendrons and ferns, a border of artemisias, and a gravel path that opens into a patio with a table and chairs. Beside the patio is a life-size stone statue of a beaver, which Nancy has surrounded with zinnias and other annuals, 'The Fairy' roses, veronicas, and ajugas, planted in concentric circles. On shady ground beside the circle garden, we grow an extensive stand of hostas, along with other plants such as a dwarf bleeding-heart (*Dicentra eximia*), the blue-flowered *Lobelia Erinus,* and *Geranium sanguineum.*

Nancy has gone from neophyte to

plant collector. In the early years, she would buy bargains, like a dozen rooted "Mollis" azaleas 5 in. high for $1.25 (which are now 5 ft. to 6 ft. tall). Starting with little plants forced Nancy to keep her own nursery, which proved to be a blessing. She could learn a plant's color and habit in the nursery before picking its permanent place in the garden. She went on every garden tour she could find; visited nurseries and the gardens of friends; made many trips to the Arnold Arboretum in Boston, which has a magnificent collection of ornamentals; and eventually joined the Arboretum, as well as the Massachusetts Horticultural Society, the Rock Garden Society and the New England Wildflower Society, groups whose members collect and share uncommon plants. We now suffer from an affliction Nancy calls plant-itis—the urge to have new plants and the problem of finding room for them.

We see the slope behind the house at considerable distances from the overlook and below, so a single specimen is often not enough to make a show. We moved a group of *Doronicum cordatum* (a 2-ft.-tall perennial with large yellow flowers) four times, in an attempt to make it stand out, before we realized that the solution was to grow a few more. Now we try to display plants in odd numbers (three, five, seven, and so on), and we've found that we need 15 or more of the smaller species to make a satisfactory show at a distance. Nancy says it's easy to put $100 into plants and never see them. She economizes by starting her own, and by dividing perennials. In the early years, she used one obliging weed, *Corydalis lutea*, as a ground cover, because it was low-growing, attractive and easy to pull up. Now she encourages the same plant, which grows 12 in. to 15 in. tall with finely cut blue-green leaves and dainty yellow flowers, to reseed and grow on the entire slope. It blooms all summer here. If it invades its neighbors, we just pull up the errant plants and throw them away. We've tried transplanting them, with limited luck.

The slope faces north, and much of it is in partial shade, so our choices are limited. Among the mainstays we've planted are sedums, which are succulent perennials; many of the epimediums, which are low spreading perennials; *Alchemilla vulgaris*, a perennial with 6-in. leaves on long stems and yellowish-green flowers; and *Bergenia cordifolia*, a low-growing perennial that stays evergreen in protected areas, though we're growing it north of its hardiness range. The astilbes are Nancy's favorite group of plants. They're disease-resistant, hardy, and attractive both in bloom and out. She especially likes 'Europa', a 20-in.-high plant with fluffy pink flowers, and 'Fanal', a carmine-red beauty. The colors of astilbe flowers

are strong enough to show at a distance, and the feathery foliage makes a good foil for neighboring flowers.

We've also planted shrubs and small trees on the slope, including many dwarf conifers that keep the garden green in winter (see photo, bottom right, facing page). Among these are *Pinus Mugo* var. *pumilio*, a compact, rounded tree; *Taxus baccata* 'Repandens', a low spreading yew; *Thuja occidentalis* 'Hetz Midget', a tiny, globe-shaped arborvitae; and *Picea Abies* 'Procumbens', a low spreading spruce. Among deciduous shrubs, we especially like *Viburnum plicatum* forma *tomentosum*, which has bright-red berries in the fall, and beautybush (*Kolkwitzia amabilis*), with its pink flowers in late spring.

Over the years, the look of the hill from close up has changed. Nancy has developed a special fondness for rock-garden plants. At the top of the slope, which is warmer and less windy than the land below, several enchanting species overwinter readily. Among these are the blue-flowered *Campanula carpatica*; the white *Dryas octopetala*, with anemone-like flowers that are followed by fluffy seed heads; and *Androsace lanuginosa*, with pink flower heads and silvery reclining leaves. Nancy also likes *Primula vulgaris*, a rapidly spreading low primrose with pale-yellow flowers, which she grows in masses.

Our gardens are now too extensive for us to maintain in a reasonable time without mulch. Every fall, we collect our fallen leaves and our neighbors', and shred enough to fill 40 to 50 large plastic bags. Early in the spring, we loosen and fertilize the soil in our plantings, and then spread at least 2 in. of shredded leaves among the plants. The mulch looks good and saves us precious time we'd otherwise have to spend on weeding. Mulching once pretty well takes care of maintenance until the following year. We think maintenance can make anyone's garden look special—edging, weeding, mulching, and keeping plants healthy and groomed show that the place is loved. If you care as we do about how your property looks, use mulch—you'll have more time for gardening.

Irrigation

We're of the opinion that it takes four things to make a successful garden: water, fertilizer, love and patience. Despite the biblical exhortation, the most important of these is water. We generally have plenty of rain in the spring and fall, but our summers can be dry and sometimes droughty. If we don't water then, we lose plants.

A good 25 years ago, we started to lay underground circuits of ¾-in. polyethylene tubing connected to permanent sprinklers. To supply water, we had to move the garden hoses from circuit to circuit, but we saved a bit of work by installing

timers to shut the water off. As the lawns and gardens grew, so did the number of circuits, and eventually we found ourselves going quietly crazy connecting and disconnecting hoses.

I automated. I built a weatherproof cabinet by the garage, collected all the sprinkler circuits inside it and supplied each one with an electrically operated valve. Two multi-station timers turn all the circuits on and off. When we used town water, the pressure would fluctuate and cause "holidays" in the sprinkler patterns. Often we discovered the trouble only when the grass turned brown, or a plant sickened. Now we have our own water supply. We fill the pond from the Charles River with a 3-HP pump and 650 ft. of 2-in.-dia. polyethylene pipe, then draw water up to the circuit cabinet with an electric pump that supplies constant pressure. We can now water every part of our property automatically, which is a great comfort to us.

The pond

In 1969, we set out to replace the back porch and ended up digging a pond. I needed a workshop, so we put a beam and posts under the roof of the porch, tore away everything else, and had a backhoe operator excavate for an addition to the basement. The operator left us with a pile of dirt and a lot of large rocks scattered on the hill—a mess. Nancy saw a chance to extend the narrow patch of level ground behind the house and alter the boring brow of the slope by using the rocks for a curving wall on the hill and the dirt for fill behind it. The job took some homemade rock-moving gear and a lot of labor, but the result was a wonderful level overlook (which we soon outlined with a hedge) that gave us a view to the bottom of the slope and across the marsh to the Charles. We call the overlook "Gasp Point" because visitors who see the innocuous front yard don't expect what they find out back. When a spring flood filled the marsh and lapped at the edge of our property, the watery view from the overlook gave us the idea for a pond at the foot of the slope, where we had removed loam for the lawn. Though we had no experience, we thought it would be a great lark to build a pond.

We outlined a figure-eight roughly 60 ft. long and 30 ft. wide. From the start, we meant to span the waist of the pond with a bridge, and we still do, although almost 20 years have gone by. A bulldozer operator cut a path to the pond site, leaving us a steep bank, which we stabilized with narrow terraces retained by wooden shingles and planted to pachysandra. (See the sidebar on p. 13 for more on holding the bank and using wooden shingles for edging.) We hired a large backhoe to start the digging, and then over

A view of the Estabrooks' property

When the Estabrooks bought this 1½-acre property in 1946, it was a vacant lot. Today the land is a mature landscape, with several prominent and harmonious features, the fruits of four decades of earthmoving, clearing, construction and planting. (Photos in the article were taken from the lettered positions.)

On railroad tracks made of 2x4s, the Estabrooks lifted 100 cu. yd. of soil up the slope and spread it 4 in. deep on the front and side yards to establish the lawn.

The author laid a semicircular stone retaining wall at the brow of the slope, extending the backyard and creating an overlook to the gardens below.

To garden on the slope, which falls 40 ft., the Estabrooks built a zigzagging grassy path from the backyard to the pond. Railroad-tie retaining walls hold the slope and level the path.
Though it faces north, the slope offers landscape interest year-round with a diverse collection of perennials, deciduous shrubs and trees, and dwarf conifers.

The author dug the pond with rented machines and sealed it with a homemade plastic liner, which remains serviceable 19 years later.

Swapping land with a neighbor, the Estabrooks eked out room by the pond for formal gardens and a sitting area.

At a turn in the grass path that descends the slope behind their house, the Estabrooks installed a concrete bench. Thirty feet below is the pond, circled by a gravel walk and flanked by an outdoor sitting area. (Taken at B on site plan.)

At close range, the slope reveals a variety of ornamentals, shrubs and small trees. At left is the dwarf arborvitae *Thuja occidentalis* 'Emerald Green', on the right is the prostrate spruce *Picea Abies* 'Nidiformis', and at top right is the purple fan-leaved Japanese maple *Acer palmatum* var. *dissectum* 'Atropurpureum'. The variegated leaves and pink flowers are *Lamium maculatum*, an often-invasive perennial member of the mint family that grows 12 in. to 18 in. high. On the north-facing slope, in partial shade, *L. maculatum* has been easy for the Estabrooks to control. (Taken at C on site plan.)

Illustrations: Staff

Carpeting the banks of a pond

We invented a gardeners' disguise for the margin of gray-PVC-plastic pond liner around the pond (see drawing below). We laid carpet scraps over the exposed PVC to wick water from the pond and planted a creeping evergreen sedum (*Sedum acre*) 3 ft. from the water. Encouraged by the moist footing, the sedum grows down the pond banks to the water's edge, covering the carpet and creating a handsome green fringe. Beyond the sedum, we planted perennials. In the foreground of the photo above (taken at D on site plan), the yellow flowers are golden poppies (*Stylophorum diphyllum*) and the pale-blue flowers are garden forget-me-nots (*Myositis sylvatica*).

—F.R.E., Jr.

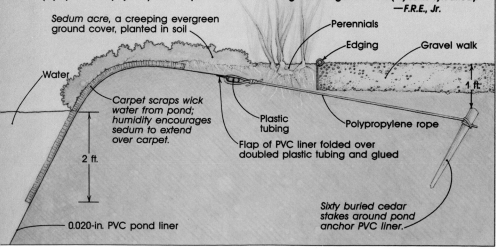

Sedum acre, a creeping evergreen ground cover, planted in soil

Perennials

Edging

Gravel walk

Water

Carpet scraps wick water from pond; humidity encourages sedum to extend over carpet.

Plastic tubing

Polypropylene rope

1 ft.

2 ft.

Flap of PVC liner folded over doubled plastic tubing and glued

0.020-in. PVC pond liner

Sixty buried cedar stakes around pond anchor PVC liner.

several weekends we rented a small four-wheel-drive, front-end loader with a detachable backhoe and finished the job ourselves. The excavation eventually produced enough dirt to make a level rim around the pond about 5 ft. wide, at a height that flowed naturally into the contours around it. The pond was 9 ft. deep at the large end and 4 ft. deep at the other. The sides were too steep to stand on, or to rake from above or below, so we smoothed them by cocking the bucket of the backhoe and swinging it back and forth.

When we finished digging, we found ourselves staring at a vessel that was strictly bank gravel, a gift from the last glacier. My closest friend said, "Only you, you dumbbell, would try to build a pond in a gravel bank!" I figured I could seal the gravel with colloidal clay. I bought a ton, in 50-lb. bags. We did our best to distribute the clay uniformly and thickly, but the slopes were far too steep and most of the clay ended up in a wet sloppy mess at the bottom. I suppose colloidal clay works as a sealer when a pond slopes gently, but it didn't help us.

I decided to make a plastic liner. In 1969, pond liners were not common items; today you can buy them in many sizes, but then you could only get rolls of sheet plastic in a limited range of widths. I chose polyvinyl chloride (PVC) because I could join pieces together easily and permanently with a solvent painted on like glue. I purchased 1,000 running feet of dark-gray PVC sheeting, 0.020 in. thick and 54 in. wide, which weighed about 600 lb. We swept off our neighbor's blacktop driveway, laid out four 80-ft. lengths, and bonded their edges, with a 2-in. overlap. Then we rolled up the assembly like a window shade on a 20-ft. stick so we could unroll it through the center of the pond without getting in the gloppy clay mess at the bottom. Once the assembly was in place, I worked around the rest of the pond, laboriously cutting and fitting pieces like a tailor, and bonding them together.

When I finished the liner, I set out to bind the perimeter. I found 500 running feet of rejected vinyl tubing about an inch or so in diameter and circled the pond with it twice. Then I rolled the PVC over the two tubes and solvent-bonded the flap with the tubing inside. This made a rugged edge, which I intended to anchor securely to keep the liner from sliding down the pond sides.

I dug a trench around the pond, 5 ft. to 6 ft. from the liner, and drove sixty 2-ft.-long cedar posts in the trench at equal spacing, with their tops 1 ft. below grade. Then I tied the liner to each stake with polypropylene rope, which doesn't rot, cutting holes in the PVC where each rope passed around the perimeter tubing. I pulled the ropes tight before knotting them and managed to smooth a lot of wrinkles in the liner. We filled the pond from a shallow homemade well and the liner held. Success.

We wanted to finish the perimeter of the pond with a border of plants, so we shoveled soil over the ropes and posts and the edge of the pond liner, but there was still about 2 ft. of exposed PVC between the dirt and the water. It seemed to me that we could start a ground cover in the soil and persuade it to spread to the water if we covered the exposed PVC with carpet that had one end in the pond. I thought the carpet would wick up moisture from the pond by capillary action and permit the ground cover to either strike roots or enjoy some relief from hot, dry weather. We used carpet scraps of all kinds, and have since found that they stay wet a foot from the pond, as I had hoped. In the soil around the pond, we planted *Sedum acre,* a creeping succulent, and it has spread luxuriantly over the carpeting to the water's edge, making a lovely green fringe around the pond. We've also buried a soaker hose around the pond, so in extremely dry weather we can irrigate the border, and we've added other plants besides sedum, including irises, purple coneflower (*Echinacea purpurea*), globe thistle (*Echinops sphaerocephalus*) and golden poppy (*Stylophorum diphyllum*). We're not certain that the carpet accounts for the sedum growing to the water, but we would like to think others will try it.

By and large, the pond has been highly successful. It's a focal point for the gardens around it, and looks great from Gasp Point. The cedar stakes and ropes have done their job for 19 years and the PVC liner has proven durable. If we had to do the project again, we'd consider using 0.030-in.-thick PVC, primarily because it might stand up a little better to falling limbs, minor vandalism and other assaults. Happily, holes in PVC are easy to repair—I cut PVC patches, bond them over the holes, and that's that. To keep out animals and leaves, I now put up a chicken-wire fence every October and take it down in March.

In the 40-odd years we've built and gardened here, our vacant lot has undergone a considerable change in appearance. The property won a Gold Medal in 1984 from the Massachusetts Horticultural Society. Somewhat to our surprise, we now find ourselves hosting garden tours, and strangers pull in off the road and ask to look around. It's a pleasure to look back and see what we've done.   □

F. Reed Estabrook, Jr. and his wife, Nancy, hope to add a bridge over the pond and a few more plants to their place in Dedham, Massachusetts.

The Estabrooks use wooden shingles to make decorative edging for paths, borders and changes in elevation, as shown here. The silver-leaved foreground plants are Artemisia Absinthium, and the shrub in bloom is royal azalea (Rhododendron Schlippenbachii). (Taken at E on site plan.)

Edging and terracing with wooden shingles

We use wooden shingles to edge paths and hold the soil on slight slopes. We buy #2 or #3 grade shingles, trim a bit off the thin ends to make them easier to install, soak them overnight in wood preservative, drain and dry them, and then drive them into the soil with a hammer. We overlap neighboring shingles by an inch or so, as shown in the photo above. If your soil is stony, you'll have to make a trench for the shingles. The shingles last eight to ten years and finally rot out, just as fenceposts do, at the junction of the moist ground and the dry air.

We've also found that shingles are handy for controlling erosion and establishing a ground cover on a steep slope. When we had a bulldozer operator cut the tractor path to the pond site, we were left with a raw bank. We drove shingles into the ground in rows 6 in. to 12 in. apart, making terraces across the bank, and planted sprigs of pachysandra along the rows. We had no trouble with erosion, and in roughly eight years the bank was thickly spread with pachysandra. Most of the shingles have since rotted or been removed, or they no longer show.   —F.R.E., Jr.

A Welcoming Entry
Redesigning a small front yard

Photos, except where noted: Monty Monsees

by Avis Rappoport Licht

Front yards ought to welcome visitors, and provide easy and inviting access from the street to the house. But all too often, the entry is hidden, with no clear path from here to there. And in most urban and suburban front yards, lawns feature prominently, clothing houses with an uninspiring apron of green. Many of my clients find grass more boring than beautiful, more work than pleasure. They want imaginative landscapes that engage them and their visitors. And if these plantings require less water than a thirsty lawn, so much the better, since we get very little rainfall here in Northern California.

When Norma Liner asked me to redesign her front yard, I was more than happy to try my hand at her small, but challenging, plot. A somewhat-derelict lawn stretched from the street back to a hedge of English laurels that butted up against a tall wood fence. The expanse was broken only by a dying plum tree and two sweet gum trees (*Liquidambar styraciflua*). On my initial visit, I spent a considerable amount of time searching for Norma's front door. My first attempt landed me next to the garbage cans, with no possibility of entering the house except through the kitchen window. After several false starts, I finally found the entry gate, hidden behind the hedge.

Norma wanted visible access from the sidewalk to the front door, lots of color year-round and reduced water use. She requested relatively low-maintenance plantings, though she wanted some opportunity to garden in the front yard.

My solution to these problems

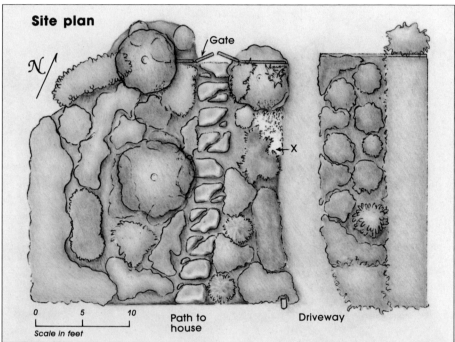

A stone path leading through a bright mass of flowers (left) creates a warm welcome to this small front yard. Tough plants such as the purple-flowered lavender along the driveway (above) require much less water and work than the lawn that once grew here. Above photo taken at X on site plan (top).

Illustration: Rosalind L. Wanke

To the left of the path (foreground), the springtime tapestry includes the blue-flowered ceanothus, pink dianthus, and pink and red freesias, and on the right, rose-red dianthus and a border of pink sea thrift. Orange California poppies continue blooming throughout the season.

was straightforward, easy to install and inexpensive. We agreed to remove the old plum tree and the lawn, and to replace them with low-water-use perennials and flowering shrubs.

A new look

The revamped garden features a sturdy path of dry-laid, river-wash stepping stones leading from the sidewalk to the front gate, now clearly visible after some of the laurels had been removed. (See site plan on p. 15.) A discontinuous path such as this gives the garden a less formal look than would a solid stretch of concrete or pavers. In a climate such as ours, where frost-heaving isn't a concern, the path provides firm footing year-round.

I chose mostly low-growing plants that fit the small scale of the garden, with a few taller ones for emphasis. I used a restrained hand to balance Norma's desire for variety and color, and my observation that simple and harmonious combinations look best. Small masses of different kinds of plants satisfied the need for variety, while creating a unified look. Our color scheme was mainly pink, purple and blue, with a few splashes of yellow, red and orange to liven up the palette.

The remainder of the laurel hedge, with its shiny, dark green leaves, makes a pleasing backdrop for the garden. A border of ceanothus (*Ceanothus griseus*), with its deep green foliage,

The delicate pink flowers and green, felted leaves of Australian fuschia, a low-growing, spreading shrub, grace the garden from fall through early spring.

mirrors the laurel leaves. This neat, compact, California native shrub is covered with beautiful, deep blue, lilac-scented flowers in the spring, and sporadic blooms in the fall. This particular cultivar tolerates some summer water as long as the soil drains well.

Near the ceanothus, correa 'Carmine

Bells' (*Correa pulchella*), a tough little evergreen shrub from Australia, is covered with fuschia-like, pink flowers from late fall through early spring. Its lingering flowers make a lovely combination with those of the ceanothus.

The large sweet gums near the house add height to the site and decorate the garden with their red, star-like leaves in the fall. Planting among the massive roots of these established trees was difficult in places, so there I mulched with 1½ in. white and black rocks, which create a striking contrast with the surrounding green foliage.

Partway up the path, a Japanese maple (*Acer palmatum*) provides a focal point, especially in the fall when its leaves turn a warm red-orange. To create an immediate effect, I purchased a large specimen maple, but to minimize costs, the rest of the plants were 1-gal. size or smaller. Partially-buried lava rocks in front of the maple accentuate a slight rise and provide a well-drained niche for plants such as saxifrage.

To avoid a cluttered look, I combined plants with similar foliage, but with overlapping or sequential flowering times. For example, along one side of the steps, I planted three low-growing plants with grass-like foliage: sea thrift (*Armeria maritima*), whose small clusters of pink flowers sit atop a green mound of foliage; mondo grass (*Ophiopogon japonicus*), a porcupine-like puff

Photo: bottom, James Katz

Yellow yarrow and orange poppies are set off by the nearby stone mulch, which serves as ground cover beneath a sweet gum tree.

of blue-green leaves; and lily turf (*Liriope muscari*), a slightly larger, green-leaved plant with purple flower spikes. Lining the other side of the steps, coralbells (*Heuchera sanguinea*) bloom first, followed by the delicate white flowers of saxifrage (*Saxifraga umbrosa* 'London Pride') and the pale pink blooms of geranium (*Geranium endressii* 'Wargrave Pink'). All of these plants have roundish, scalloped-edged leaves.

To round out the spring bloom, I planted many bulbs of narcissus, freesia, crocus and anemone (*Anemone coronaria*). Quite obligingly, their foliage dies back a short while after flowering, leaving room for the summer-bloomers—lantana (*Lantana montevidensis*), penstemon, verbena, Mexican primrose (*Oenothera berlandieri*), California poppy and lavender. In the fall, the bright red blooms of California fuchsia (*Zaushneria californica*) are set off against its gray-green foliage. This mat-forming plant is a favorite of hummingbirds. And flowers of red penstemons, orange and yellow lantana, yellow and pink yarrows, orange Iceland poppies and pink geraniums stick their heads up through the brightly-colored, fallen leaves of the maple and sweet gum.

Looking back

Four years after planting, the advantages of the new garden, as well as a few problems, have become evident. On the plus side, the garden constant-

The richly-colored leaves of a Japanese maple and a taller sweet gum create a lovely focus in early fall.

ly displays showy blooms and thrives with minimal water. It has truly provided a path out of boredom. Though the perennials need some dead-heading to keep them neat, the garden requires little work compared to the ever-present demands of weekly lawn mowing and watering. Pruning in the spring and fall, along with occasional snips the rest of the year, keeps the plants renewed. Beyond that, the garden requires only

periodic irrigation and fertilizing.

We have been disappointed, however, in some of the vigorous, drought-hardy and long-lived plants, which also have proved to be invasive and sometimes scruffy. In fact, I've yet to find one of them that knows its bounds. The most notorious invader is the lovely Mexican primrose. Its lavender-pink, delicate flowers and profuse blooms recommend it highly, but it spreads everywhere and looks awful in the fall. Trimming it back regularly helps keep it in bounds.

Another such plant is California fuchsia. It continues to bloom after almost every other flower is gone. But talk about shoddy—when it blooms, this plant really needs some camouflage to cover its leggy stems and sparse foliage. Interplanting it with other low-growing plants such as dianthus 'Tiny Rubies' or twinspur (*Diascia rigescens*) creates a carpet of green around its base. But, in truth, an eye that overlooks small problems such as this is the best solution of all.

If you're accustomed to the reliability of an evergreen front lawn, this style of garden may challenge your way of thinking. But I'd encourage you to try it. With an ever-changing palette of flowering plants, the anticipation of what's to come brings as much pleasure as an appreciation of what's blooming today. □

Avis Rappoport Licht is a landscape designer in Woodacre, CA.

Exuberant plantings extend an irresistible invitation to explore the garden. The arbor over the front walk is heavy-laden with an unusual climbing form of 'The Fairy' rose that seems to arise from a blue hydrangea. (Photo taken at A on site plan, p. 21.)

Creating Paradise
A garden that feeds the soul

by Ruth Rohde Haskell

Walk down the sanded drive, step through the picket gate, and you enter another world—a blend of Southern France and rural Dixie with overtones of the tropics. Ryan Gainey's romantic cottage garden in Decatur, Georgia, is one of the South's best-known treasures. Uniting his skills as artist, designer, gardener and plantsman, Gainey has created an oasis that's highly personal and full of wit and charm. Even though you're only a block from a major thoroughfare that runs straight to downtown Atlanta, a few miles away, the noise of the city stops short at the street. In the hot stillness of a summer day, you're surrounded by lush greenery, and birdsong is the predominant sound.

Every garden has to have a philosophy, a reason why it exists. Gainey's garden exists to be a bit of heaven on earth for its creator.

Fulfilling personal desires

The garden occupies three lots that belonged to a family with a nursery business. Four of the original greenhouses still stand, and Gainey uses them for forcing bulbs, producing topiary and housing his collection of rhizomatous begonias and tropical plants. The garden is divided into a series of rooms—front garden, visitor's garden, dry wall garden, terrace, barn garden, vegetable garden and oval garden, among others (see the site plan on p. 21)—each with its own character and role. Garden ornaments and red cedar arbors, pergolas and trellises abound. And everywhere you turn there are places to sit, inviting you to observe and enjoy the garden.

The exuberant plantings and rustic cedar structures make the garden seem mature, but portions are less than ten years old, and Gainey continues to alter his design. Like many successful gardens, his started without a plan. "I wanted to express myself artistically," he says, "but I had no concept of what I was going to do with this property. I didn't even know any plants. I'd studied horticulture and landscape design, but I'd never created a garden. I had been inspired by a good college professor, but, you know, you can have all the inspiration in the world, and it just sits in there until you do something with it; it doesn't mean anything."

To educate himself, Gainey sought gardening books that appealed to his eye, such as Peter Coats' *Plants for Connoisseurs*, rather than books that were primarily practical. He chose plants that were wonderful to look at and tried them to see if they'd grow in his climate.

Gainey wants enclosed spaces, and the separate garden areas, many with surrounding hedges, walls or

In a warm-colored and striking combination, red and yellow species tulips (*Tulipa acuminata* and *T. clusiana*) mingle with eastern columbine and an underplanting of yellow violas and native biennial senecio.

plantings, fulfill this need. Continuity and the spirit of a place are also important to him, so he kept the open spaces of the property and made them garden rooms. Gainey also reused materials he found on the property, such as the paving stones in his perennial border. "I didn't know what I was going to do with them, but I dug them up one day, put them in a pile, tilled, got the soil to what I thought was wonderful (which wasn't), and then I laid out this pattern. I was going to have borders, herbaceous borders, which is an absurd idea in the South because of the length of our season." The grand borders Gainey originally envisioned gave way to mixed ones of shrubs, perennials and annuals.

Gainey continues to refine his garden. "To make what you have work successfully for you, you have to continually work with it. I've made a lot of wonderfully intuitive mistakes that turned out to be successes." The oval garden is a good example. Originally, he had flowers in the center with a grass walkway around them. Later, he filled the center with grass and surrounded it with the gold and golden-variegated plants that he loves.

Developing a garden philosophy

Gainey believes that we all spend our lives searching for paradise and that gardeners strive to create their own version. He deplores untidiness and disorder, considering them the results of an uncaring attitude. Everyone should try to make his property inviting, he thinks.

Gainey considers Vaux-le-Vicomte, the 18th-century French garden of topiary and water, to be the supreme earthly paradise. Clipped, patterned and orderly, Vaux-le-Vicomte is the ultimate expression of cultivated, civilized nature, Gainey believes, because man is completely in control. Gainey finds the romantic English landscape garden Stourhead equally wonderful. Both are far cries from his own vine-swathed cottage and garden of buxom plants that can't keep to their beds.

Gainey bemoans the fact that so many American gardens peak in spring, and he continually searches for plants that have fall or winter interest. Shrubs and annuals are his great loves; he uses herbaceous plants almost as supplements. Nothing is so powerful or enriching to Gainey as foliage. He finds the colors in new growth breathtaking. Those variations of green, red,

Formal beds enliven the vegetable garden. Bronze-leaved lettuces cluster in the foreground. (Photo taken at B on site plan.)

amber and brown are the real colors, he contends. A plant's flowers can be just as subtle as they want to be—the more subtle they are, the better he loves them.

Is it a surprise to hear a self-professed plantsman declare he loves annuals? Maybe the garden works so successfully because it's unexpected, with tightly clipped topiaries in one area and billowing flowers in the next, classic Italian urns placed before bark-encrusted cedar arbors, native species growing cheek by jowl with large-leaved tropicals. "After all," he says, "isn't the idea of paradise exotic?"

Design advice

When asked what advice he would give to people designing their own very personal gardens, Gainey has lots to recommend. Several themes continually resurface: know your limitations as well as your needs, use restraint, and integrate the elements.

"You only need a garden as big as you can afford to make and to maintain in a manner that is self-expressive and has in it the things that you personally feel are important to what a garden is. That garden should be as close to and as intimately involved with your house as any other room in your house. It isn't a place that you go to; it is a place that you go into and out of as you go into and out of your house. It needs to be that integrated."

However large or small your garden space, Gainey says, you can subdivide it any way that fits your needs and your site. Then decide what you'd like to have *here*, and how you're going to walk *there*. In a very small place, you can have only a limited number of things, so you need to choose them carefully, place them carefully, and have nothing else. What you end up practicing, Gainey points out, is restraint.

A garden needs certain features. One is open space. Another is water—a small pool or the sound of moving water. Third, a place to sit, uncovered or covered. A covered seat introduces the idea of a pergola or arbor and the opportunity to have plants that grow upwards and climb. Finally, it's important to have detached structures or outbuildings. "I don't care if it's a folly or an outhouse," Gainey says. "It's just another element that exists. That's where the idea of the gazebo comes from."

So you have water and grass and space and terraces, and maybe a change of grade with steps, but

A flagstone path and a glimpse of the garden room beyond beckon strollers between two urns perched on stacks of clay pots. (Photo taken at C on site plan.)

The colors and textures of new leaves enliven the garden in spring. Here, a new leaf of rice paper plant *(Tetrapanax papyriferus)* contrasts with older foliage. Root-hardy in Gainey's Zone 7 garden and a self-sower as well, rice paper plant perpetuates itself without much work on the gardener's part.

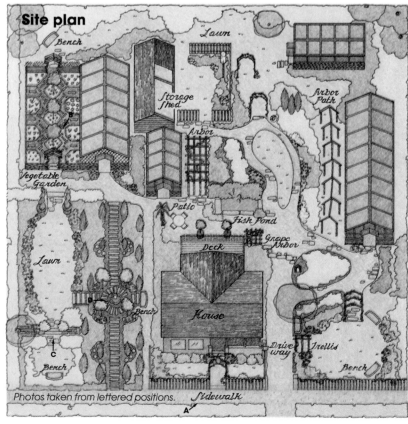

Site plan

Bench
Lawn
Storage Shed
Arbor Path
Arbor
Vegetable Garden
Patio
Fish Pond
Grape Arbor
Lawn
Deck
Bench
House
Bench
C
Bench
Driveway
Trellis
Bench

Photos taken from lettered positions.
Sidewalk
A

Illustration: Natalie Forsberg Siegel; photo, above left: Ruth Rohde Haskell

foxgloves

bronze fennel

alstroemeria

iris

milk thistle
(*Silybum marianum*)

Spiraea × *bumalda*
'Goldflame'

Leaf shapes and colors provide variety in this corner of the garden, while the flowers share similar shades of rose-pink.

the need for certain features leaves open what the steps or the terrace are made of, or what kind of fish go into the pool, or what material is used for the bench or the arbor. Those are choices for you, the gardener, and they will be dictated by your location and climate, your house, your tastes, and what plants and materials you like.

Knowing how and when to use plants is a skill that can be developed by observation and by practice. Gainey is regarded as something of a wizard when it comes to combining plants. The key, he believes, is being able to really *see*. Seeing in three dimensions is vital to designing a good garden. "I'll teach a person anything I know, but I cannot teach someone how to see. You have to learn that for yourself."

Maintaining and perpetuating the garden

You shouldn't have more garden than you can take care of, Gainey insists, though any garden is likely to be more work during its first few years. To begin with, you must

let a garden get to the point where you want it, then do what you have to do to maintain it. After three to five years, you'll know how the garden grows, and what needs to be done to keep it up.

Plant selection is a partial answer to keeping maintenance manageable. Although Gainey grows many plants for their associations—for what they mean to him—he also chooses plants that get along without much work on his part. For instance, he lets rice paper plants (*Tetrapanax papyriferus*) come up wherever they want, from roots or seeds, because their exotic leaves are usually welcome and the plants need no care. If they appear where they're unwanted, he digs them out. "I don't do a thing to those rice paper plants except cut them down to the ground in the wintertime. That's all, and then back up they come. I love *Macleaya cordata,* the plume poppy, because it's one of those travelers, too. Both are primarily textural plants. Even though the *Macleaya* blooms, it's really for the foliage that I grow it. The leaves catch the light wonderfully."

Rather than bedding out, Gainey beds in—a phrase he coined—which means he sets bedding plants into the garden, where they look as if they arose naturally. Much of the bedding in takes place in the winter months, which is a superb time to garden in Georgia. Gainey sets out cool-season annuals and biennials that were started in late summer or fall. By spring, he has big, healthy plants that bloom well and early. Winter planting is especially effective with biennials, such as sweet William and foxglove, or with the tender perennial sweet alyssum. When the cool-season plants begin to wane, Gainey pulls them and replaces them with summer flowers. This practice helps give him an all-year garden, and it spreads the work out into parts of the year that are generally spent indoors.

Gainey largely avoids insect damage by allowing the plants enough room in which to grow. Sometimes his garden is bothered by whitefly or spider mites. He believes that the more you create a garden with the plants' needs in mind, the less work you have and the fewer insect or disease problems that are likely to crop up. You also need to choose your plants carefully, finding those that don't suffer from insects or disease. "But, you know, it's hard not to have hollyhocks," he muses.

"I think plants become more susceptible to pestilence because of being cultivated. When they're out under what might be considered adverse conditions to us, they actually are stronger, better plants and produce more flowers than if they're cultivated. Hollyhocks are a good example. You can see them where they grow in the south of France with a little bit of sun, in the sand, no cultivation, no water, no nothing. They bloom their heads off, they stand up tall, and they don't get spider mites. Or if they do, they don't get them as bad. Same thing with cornflower, the annual *Centaurea*. On its own, it's wonderful; but if you cultivate it, it just becomes a floppy, vegetative mess."

So Ryan Gainey's maxim for a well-designed garden also makes for a healthier garden: wherever you live, find what works there, bring in from other places the plants that are compatible horticulturally and artistically, and make a wonderful garden.   □

Ruth Rohde Haskell is the former executive editor of Fine Gardening. *She gardens in New Haven, Connecticut.*

Stone pavers radiate like spokes of a wheel from a centerpiece of purple pansies and a lattice-decorated urn. In the background, a cast iron bench under a cedar arbor invites visitors to enjoy the view. (Photo taken at D on site plan.)

The venerable wisteria and the old roses at this Vancouver house reminded the author of the Nantucket gardens of her childhood. Since buying the house, Joan Brink and her husband have transformed the small front yard (above and right) into a colorful cottage garden.

A nostalgic ship-rail picket fence borders the front yard, offering passersby a glimpse of flax, California poppies, roses and pansies (below and left). The fence can barely contain the abundance of forget-me-nots and dame's rocket in this yard. The soft colors of spring will give way to brighter plants as the season advances.

A City Cottage Garden

Flowers and fragrance for nostalgic charm

by Joan Brink

When my husband, Joel, and I began to plan a garden for our house in Vancouver, British Columbia, we discovered that we had three major requirements to fulfill. I wanted to create a cottage garden reminiscent of the Nantucket gardens of my childhood. And having just returned from a five-year stay in Italy, we wanted to grow plants that we had encountered there. Finally, we envisioned combining the gardening styles we'd learned in New England and Italy with the splendid flora of the Pacific Northwest.

Although a tall order, the mixture of plants and styles worked because our narrow lot naturally divided itself into three areas, each with different light levels and microclimates. These small gardens allow us to diversify our plant collection. One of the backyard gardens is inspired by an Italian courtyard, and another is planted in native woodland ferns and flowers. Surrounded by a white picket fence and packed with flowers, the front yard fits my definition of a cottage garden.

The garden didn't exist when we bought our house in the 1970s—there was only a lawn with a few shrubs, roses and several trees. It came as no surprise to me, though, that the gabled, shingle-style house covered with wisteria and with two old 'Dr. W. Van Fleet' roses in the yard attracted my attention. It called up a vision of a cottage garden—a garden on a human scale, which, though small, has flowers in abundance and welcomes passersby to participate in its beauty. My grandmother, who had a small garden on Cape Cod, had shared her love of cultivated flowers and her knowledge of native Massachusetts plant species with me. Over the years, I developed an avid interest in cottage gardens and wildflowers.

The first five years we lived in the house, however, our small (33-ft. × 120-ft.), rectangular city lot remained little changed. Then, in 1980, we moved to Florence, Italy, where we lived for five years while Joel worked on a fellowship. Our gardening experiences in Italy were incorporated into our Vancouver garden design when we returned home in 1985.

The front garden

The south-facing front yard was a perfect place to grow the sun-loving perennials and annuals that my grandmother grew. This garden began as a collection of plants. But as it took shape, I began to consider the design—the color, size and arrangement of the plants—and slowly the garden took on its present cottage look.

We started working on the front garden as soon as we moved back to British Columbia. We had few existing plants to work with—the two old roses, a large flowering quince, the magnificent wisteria vine and a hydrangea tree that overhung the front steps. We began digging flower beds. Eventually, we did away with most of the front lawn by running beds around the perimeter of the yard and along either side of the central walk. We wanted to plant each bed intensively, so we built up the soil, which was acidic and, fortunately, already high in humus. We added compost some years, mushroom manure and leaf mold other years, and one year we put down a layer of seaweed. After the garden was planted, we switched from digging the compost into the beds to spreading it around the plants. Because of my predilection for gathering seeds, the first plants I put in this garden were varieties that had escaped local gardens to grow in nearby vacant fields and along roadsides. I simply scattered these seeds in the newly-dug beds, and they grew well on their own.

Early in the season, front garden plants range in color from lavender through white, rose and yellow. Forget-me-nots (*Myosotis*), feverfew (*Matricaria*), yellow Welsh poppies (*Meconopsis cambrica*) and poppies (*Papaver somniferum*), foxgloves (*Digitalis*), mallow (*Malva moschata*), silvery rose campion (*Lychnis coronaria*) and dame's rocket (*Hesperis matronalis*) thrive. They form the cool colors of the garden's varied palette. Because these plants seed so prolifically each year, in the spring we thin and rearrange their seedlings against the background of perennial plants such as campanula, Shasta daisies and hardy geraniums.

For example, I arrange masses of the biennial forget-me-nots in staggered rows along the front walk and in a central, circular bed. Their soft blue haze complements the yellow Welsh poppies and the orange geums that bloom in April and May. The forget-me-nots then drop their seed in time to be pulled up in late May to make room for annuals, which I set out by the first of June. One of my favorites is flowering tobacco (*Nicotiana*), which blooms from July through September. By fall, new forget-me-nots have grown in nooks and crannies of the garden, ready to be transplanted. These will bloom the following year.

After returning from Tuscany, we planted seeds of Italian plant species—masses of European field poppy (*Papaver rhoeas*) and blue bugloss (*Anchusa italica*), both of which are annual self-seeders. In June and July, waves of cinnabar-red poppies are a real crowd stopper. Bugloss is a brilliant blue wildflower. In our Pacific seaside climate, bugloss grows 5 ft. to 6 ft. tall and blooms from May to frost. Wild fennel, rosemary, varieties of rock rose and broom (*Spartium junceum*), with its stalks of yellow flowers similar in appearance to sweet peas, also found places in the garden. I added some old-fashioned roses: the shrub roses 'Golden Wings', 'Goldbusch' and 'Nevada', the grandiflora 'Dainty Bess', and *Rosa rugosa* 'Alba'.

The year we returned from Italy, I also started to indulge my love for bellflowers (*Campanula*) and hardy geraniums. Both plants thrive in our mild climate. They contribute blue and lavender colors to the garden during June, countering the pinks and yellows of the roses and the reds of the poppies.

Framing the front garden—For several years we wanted to enclose the garden with an attractive, low picket fence. We envisioned using the Nantucket ship-rail fence, but it was a style unknown in the Northwest (see photo on p. 24). Fortunately, we had carried back a piece of the distinctive ship-rail molding from our last trip to Nantucket and were able to have the 100 ft. of fencing we needed duplicated by a local carpenter. We set the picket fence 1½ ft. back from the sidewalk. Our final artistic touch was to plant the narrow strip outside the fence with a hedge of dwarf

A dramatic display of potted, white-flowering plants includes regal lily, schizanthus, petunias, geraniums and a glazed pot of water containing a white water lily.

'Munstead' lavender. Its color is a rich purple, and its fragrance is one I associate with the south of France, where lavender is grown in fields for the perfume industry. With the gleaming white fence in place, an elegant frame had been added to our impressionistic garden.

The back garden

Our stay in Italy, the land of piazzas and courtyard gardens, had given us a desire to pave a space that would give us a sitting area to use during our exquisite summers. Before we moved to Italy, we grew vegetables in the northwest corner of the backyard, because it was the only sunny space on our back lot. After our return, we drew up a plan for a circular area and forever after labelled it "the piazza." In reality, a piazza is an open, paved space where outdoor markets are set up and people gather. Our piazza is a place where our friends can gather, and we can enjoy the garden. The final touch was the addition of a curving pathway leading

from the house to the sitting area. In cool contrast to the sun-baked piazza is the woodland garden, near the north side of the house.

The woodland garden—Three cedars, planted very close together, reminded us of the cypresses that form many of the "sacred groves" of Tuscany. Our trees, like those groves, have an architectural, almost cathedral-like quality. In the shade of the cedar grove and the house we planted natives of the Northwest, or plants that are adapted to these conditions, a combination of ferns, perennials and blooming shrubbery.

We planted British Columbia woodland ferns: sword fern (*Polystichum munitum*), deer fern (*Blechnum spicant*), lady fern (*Athyrium filix-femina*), northern maidenhair (*Adiantum pedatum*) and ostrich fern (*Matteuccia*). For color, foliage and height, we planted rhododendrons in all shades but red. To visually soften the edges of the beds in this area, we used groupings of beach-smoothed stones that I collected on my walks along the ocean. Later, clumps of trilliums, wild and cultivated bleeding-hearts, saxifrages, ajuga, starflowers (*Trientalis latifolia*), western spring-beauty (*Montia sibirica*), Solomon's-seal (*Polygonatum multiflorum*) and windflowers (*Anemone blanda*) found places beneath the cedars.

We enrich the soil in this area by mulching with leaf mold, which we collect from nearby woods. Hostas are a perfect edging for the paths, forming a transition to the sunny area where broom, lilies, roses, Japanese anemones, campanulas and perennial geraniums have their home. In the intermediate zone between full shade and sun, a group of blue Tibetan poppies (*Meconopsis betonicifolia*) and primroses (*Primula japonica*) have made a tentative stand. The poppies, growing 3 ft. tall and having sky-blue flowers, need a generous amount of leaf mold each year. They are probably one of the more pampered plants in the garden. I love blue flowers and poppies, so I find this combination irresistible.

The 7-ft.-tall cedar and lath fence we originally built to enclose the backyard had deteriorated by the time we returned to Vancouver. We decided to duplicate the original fence because cedar is a native wood and weathers well. The fence provides a perfect trellis for my clematis collection: *Clematis montana* 'Grandiflora', *C.* × *jackmannii*, 'Nellie Moser', 'Candida' and 'Vyvyan Pennell'. These ensure complete privacy for our piazza, surrounding us with luxuriant and colorful blossoms throughout most of the summer.

The piazza—The ground in the backyard had degenerated into a series of holes and uneven ridges during our absence, so we hired a professional landscaper to grade the area, rebuild the fence, install a lawn and lay the

The cedar and lath fence surrounding the Brinks' back-yard became a trellis for clematis. The vine-covered fence provides privacy and a colorful background for perennial geraniums, campanulas, and lady's-mantle.

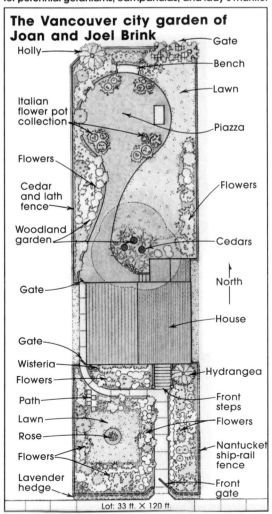

The Vancouver city garden of Joan and Joel Brink

- Holly
- Gate
- Bench
- Lawn
- Italian flower pot collection
- Piazza
- Flowers
- Flowers
- Cedar and lath fence
- Woodland garden
- Cedars
- Gate
- North
- House
- Gate
- Wisteria
- Hydrangea
- Flowers
- Path
- Front steps
- Lawn
- Flowers
- Rose
- Nantucket ship-rail fence
- Flowers
- Lavender hedge
- Front gate

Lot: 33 ft. × 120 ft.

Photo, top: Joan Brink; illustration, Vince Babak

A small, circular courtyard (above), inspired by the piazzas (public squares) the author saw in Italy, is a gathering place for family and friends. Hostas, maidenhair ferns, azaleas and rhododendrons grow in the author's small, woodland garden (below).

paving stones. For the piazza we chose heritage stones, concrete aggregate paving blocks with a warm, brick-like color that enlivens the garden during gray, winter days. We've never regretted hiring the work out, because it was executed with care and precision within the space of just a week.

The shady part of the backyard garden merges into this sunny, circular piazza where we've planted some of the same perennials used in the front yard. The piazza is edged with bellflower (*Campanula*), lady's-mantle (*Alchemilla vulgaris*) and more hardy geraniums. It is flanked on the north by old holly trees that I am gradually shaping into standards. Between the hollies we set a semi-circular, concrete bench, reminiscent of ones we saw in Italy. It is backed by a wall of clipped Mexican orange (*Choisya*) set off with roses and pots of geraniums.

An area under the eastern-most holly turned out to be a microclimate—an unexpected hot spot in the garden. Here we planted a Spanish broom, rosemary and creeping thyme—all plants with perfumes redolent of Mediterranean settings. A clump of a Ligtu hybrid Peruvian lily (*Alstroemeria*) has proven particularly successful here. We rely on pots of annuals—marguerites, lobelia, petunias and violas—to carry the blooming period from early summer to the end of the season. I move the potted plants around during the summer to mask bloomed-out areas bordering the piazza.

I used to change the color scheme of my potted annuals from year to year. Then one year we had almost exclusively white potted flowers. We planted large terra cotta tubs of marguerites, white violas, and regal lilies, and had a tub of water containing white water lilies. These, combined with our traditional pots of fuchsias and geraniums, gave a splendid show. Since then, I continue to use white flowers and to accent them with the geraniums that I hold over each winter in my basement light room.

Fragrance, color and texture

Over time, fragrance has become important to our design—we associate fragrances with our gardening memories and with other places we have lived. After we discovered this, we started consciously including flowers and shrubs with evocative scents. A rock rose (*Cistus*) planted by the front steps gives off a pungent smell year-round that, for me, is a sensory express trip to the hills of Tuscany and Sardinia, while *Rosa rugosa* brings back pleasant memories of a Nantucket garden.

My love of rose campion and its subsequent over-abundance got me into trouble with color. I have long been infatuated with this plant's silvery-gray foliage, which calms its hot magenta blooms. But nearby, I had an expanding stand of scarlet beebalm (*Monarda didyma*) planted to attract hummingbirds. These two plants in the same small garden produced a serious color discordance. I had to eliminate the beebalm, hummingbirds notwithstanding. Because of this experience, I became more sensitive to the delicate color harmonies of successful cottage gardening.

With this in mind, I planted wormwood (*Artemisia*) for its silvery leaf color. As the plants filled in, they became a shimmering foil for the hotter tones of late summer flowers. I also now allow feverfew to self-seed so that its lacy, white blossoms are interspersed with the reds and oranges of June and July. The feverfew gives way to clumps of Shasta daisies and silver artemisias during July and August. By using an abundance of white-flowered and silver-leaved plants, I have found that all but the hottest reds can flower pleasingly with the blues, purples and pinks of my garden.

I like to group plants with various leaf colors, shapes and textures to create eye-catching combinations. I first noticed textures when a meadow rue (*Thalictrum aquilegifolium*) made its way into the garden and planted itself between a tree peony and *Geranium ibericum*. The meadow rue's dainty, complex leaves dance above the large, simpler leaves of the tree peony and the pinnate, maple-like leaves of the geranium. This combination of shapes caught my eye, and the endless potential of textures opened new gardening possibilities. I planted lady's-mantle, whose beautiful, round, cup-like leaves hold jewel-like droplets of water. Other plants I like for their texture include hostas, yellow iris (*Iris pseudacorus*), lamb's-ears (*Stachys byzantina*) and acanthus.

Joan Brink believes delicate color harmonies are integral to her success with cottage gardening.

Maintenance

Summer—Although the front garden is small, its maintenance occupies a good deal of my spare time during the growing season. I stake the taller plants because of the great heights they reach—some grow up to 6 ft. tall. In midsummer, I spend a couple of days a week dead-heading, transplanting and removing spent plants to make room for those coming into bloom.

The backyard requires constant raking and sweeping of tree leaves from the perennial beds and piazza. When perennials stop blooming, they are quickly cut back and filled in with blooming annuals.

Autumn—I clean up the garden in stages. I do a first cleanup in front and back in late summer, followed by a second cleanup after the first frost. I compost soft plant debris and send the hardwood trimmings to our city mulching program. In October, after the flower beds are cleaned out, I move pots of rhododendrons and azaleas into strategic locations in the yard as visual focal points.

Spring—Cleanup starts again in February, when I rake the remaining leaves from perennial beds and cut back the roses. This is followed by the late spring ritual of re-arranging plants, adding compost and planting flowers.

Gardening in a climate that sustains such a broad range of plants has been fulfilling. While our front garden remains a visual feast during its blooming period and provides a bounty of cutflowers, the back garden has become a summertime extension of our home. For us, the joys of gardening are now combined with the joys of living in the garden we have created. □

Joan Brink is an artist who weaves baskets of historic design in Vancouver, British Columbia.

A Garden Graced by Age

The natural touch shapes a beloved refuge

Half-hidden by the tall blades and vivid flowers of the butterfly iris 'Golden Lady', the author reaps a floral harvest. Her 33-year-old garden is now open to the public, and friends and volunteers shoulder most of the maintenance.

by Hortense Miller

Not so many years ago, a garden as casual as mine was scarcely admitted to be a garden by many people. Some wanted it formal. Some wanted it to look like the well-watered gardens they knew back East. Some just wanted it to show it was regulated by man. But if you fell asleep in this garden and awoke suddenly, you would know you were in southern California immediately. The garden suits, it fits, it looks right, as no man-dominated landscape ever can.

Because my garden has been under one owner for 33 years, it is unusual in southern California where people change houses and change again, tearing out their predecessors' gardens to start over. Most gardens are very small, and getting smaller. People can't imagine that what they buy in a gallon pot can cover a wall, grow two stories high, blanket a hillside.

As my garden matures, it grows more beautiful. The way plants dispose themselves and weave together into a great mass can be seen only when they've had time to do it. A twisted juniper with malviscus vine winding through, a red hibiscus joining in and

All photos, except where noted: Chris Curless

In the more formal part of the garden near the house, a path leads past daylilies and a white star jasmine to a gate in the bamboo fence, which keeps hungry deer at bay.

The garden is 2½ acres of land undulating up and down on one side of "Boat Canyon." (There are no boats in Boat Canyon, as there is nothing boatable about it.) The garden is steep enough to need 400 steps or so. There is a view of the Pacific about 500 ft. below and a bit of the town visible between me and the ocean. To the west and north is an old barbed wire fence, invisible but there, along the old lines of 1837 that mark the boundaries of the neighboring property, a huge tract of undeveloped land called the San Joaquin Ranch. When the fog is low, it comes up the canyon like a snake following its curves. When the fog is higher, the other side of the canyon can't be seen. To go down into that little canyon in the fog is to have a world to yourself with no sound whatsoever, except, perhaps, the song of a sparrow.

The loveliest time in the garden is when the sun gets far enough west to put the opposite side of the canyon in blue or purple shadow. On this side the eucalyptus leaves glitter as shafts of light go through the trees and through the bushes that are clumped around them. Flowers are back-lit.

Much of this garden is unwatered chaparral, glorious with wildflowers after nature sends fire through the brush. Chaparral is made up of plants that have adapted to dry summers and wet winters (but not very wet nor very cold—there is no frost). Only the Pacific Ocean and the west winds save the land from being a desert. Faced with eight months of drought in the summer, chaparral plants cannot grow large; the highest are 10 ft. tall. To save water, they have small, hard, varnished leaves, or skeletonized leaves or leaves that are white with meal or hair. Some plants lose their leaves entirely in the summer and go to sleep. Many gardeners cannot adapt to this. They come to California for its beauty and then change it by insisting on green year-round. I grow impatient in my old age with slow learners.

a pink morning-glory going to the top, then hanging down—these are things we can't arrange. They just happen.

I never expected to be stylish. But quite suddenly the homemade fences, the mulch from the shredder-grinder, the common flowers, the wandering paths, the size of things (big) are all appreciated. Several years ago I opened the garden to the public. The number of visitors has grown from a trickle to a steady stream. (For information on visiting, see the box on p. 32.)

The land

Before I moved to Laguna Beach, I never had more than a city lot—or what is left of a city lot after a house is built on it—for a garden. I had always been distracted with teaching or traveling. But soon after I moved here from Chicago, I found myself alone at the age of 50, with land enough for a big garden in a canyon with year-round growing weather.

A purple cranesbill (Geranium incanum) and a velvet rose (Aeonium canariense) with red-tipped rosettes find their niche atop a retaining wall of broken concrete. The wall holds back the soil, making gardening on the steep slopes possible.

Building the garden

As I made my garden, I didn't interfere with the lay of the land. The country was beautiful beyond anything I could have devised, and the way the light slanted over it was enchanting. I merely followed natural paths back and forth over the hills, put railroad-tie steps in where needed, bought plants that would grow (or would not), gave them water and left them alone.

Framed by the trunks of two sugar gum eucalyptus trees, the author's garden meanders down the side of a California canyon. Once perceived as too wild, in its maturity the garden has become appreciated for its natural-looking plantings.

Thirty-three years ago there was none of this feeling of human pressure that we now have here. I simply started a garden around the house. Don Estep, a good and sensitive gardener, came once a week, bringing his choice of plants and putting them in. We divided the land around the house between us. He took the more civilized areas and I the wilder ones.

We made foot paths along the contours of the hills, built steps, extended water lines. We worked down the hill in front of the house, planting around the coastal chaparral, and leaving it intact. We held back hills by building retaining walls of broken concrete, which curve with the hillside. We also used railroad ties for retaining walls; some we laid down full-length, some we cut and stood on end.

An 8-ft. bamboo fence that we put up ourselves keeps part of the garden safe from deer. Without this protection we could not have roses, geraniums, Japanese anemones, Mexican evening primroses, daylilies or a host of other flowers deer eat. The fence follows the curves of the hills and lasts as well as a wooden fence as long as the bamboo doesn't touch the earth.

We grind everything cut in the garden—everything that will grind—and return it to the paths or to the plants. The chips are much more pleasant to walk on than the bare soil, and there is no problem with mud. We do not keep a compost pile; we just spread the raw materials on the ground.

Plants and animals

Many of the plants that thrive in this warm, dry, frost-free climate are unfamiliar to people in other parts of the country, even to people in other parts of California. Our plants are lovely, but no more so than others—just different.

I like common flowers that can take care of themselves—asters, goldenrods and sunflowers; Mexican daisies and tree daisies and tree dahlias; sages, tecomas, cistus and artemisias. Many of them are plants of the chaparral; they need no encouragement.

VISITING HORTENSE MILLER'S GARDEN

Hortense Miller's garden is open to the public. Visitors can arrange guided tours by calling the Laguna Beach Recreation Department at 714-497-0716 (reservations accepted no more than six weeks in advance). The guides are trained by the Friends of the Hortense Miller Garden, a membership organization that also publishes a quarterly newsletter and a book entitled *The Garden Writings of Hortense Miller*, an anthology of articles from the newsletter. Dues are $15 per year. The book sells for $9.50 ppd. Write to the Friends of the Hortense Miller Garden, P.O. Box 742, Laguna Beach, CA 92652.

To add interest to the garden during the summer, when many of the native plants are at rest, I have also brought in adapted foreigners. Australia has given us many bushes that are curiously deer-proof: hakea, correa, grevillea, melaleucas and the marvelous acacias. South Africa has contributed bulbs: the naked-lady amaryllis and crinums (which have pink, amaryllis-like flowers perched atop 5-ft tall, leafless stalks), the lilies of the Nile and the bulbinella (a love!) with its clear yellow, hyacinth-like flowers. Chile gave us the spectacular puyas, with their 8-ft. stalks of blue-green flowers stiff and uncompromising among stabbing foliage.

Vines that flower are a particular delight, especially those that hang in a swaying curtain of bloom like the yellow cat claw or the blue morning-glory—real displays. I like to see them find their route to the top of things. It seems intelligent, that searching. The way the Mexican red trumpet uses its five-fingered tendrils to seek out and hold on is unbelievable.

Many of the vines in my garden have grown enormous over the years. Probably the largest of all is the yellow mermaid rose, *Rosa bracteata*, which gets along over the steepest hill a lot better than we do and roots wherever she touches ground.

Fragrance has been important in this garden, perhaps because the chaparral shrubs are so fragrant. On a chilly morning, the furnace pulls in air from the garden, warms it, and blows it into the house so that you are immersed in a perfume—just what, you can't say.

I like animals in the garden. A garden without animals is like a florist's refrigerator. There used to be more animals and a greater variety of birds. "Progress" has done them in. We still have deer, ground squirrels, a raccoon or two, a bobcat now and then, lizards and snakes, including the rattler. I feed a pair of ravens. Occasionally a vulture comes in. A roadrunner turns up. Hawks and owls are still about, and mourning doves, and the usual towhees, thrashers, scrub jays, house linnets—but somehow not many.

For two years there have been 50 valley quail in the garden. For 20 years or so they were gone from these hills, and a call was never heard. Now some have come back. A little victory! □

The barbed leaves of furcroyas (agave relatives) pierce the late afternoon sky. Across the canyon, the native chaparral covers the rolling hillsides, still green after ample winter rains.

Hortense Miller gardens in Laguna Beach, California.

Like a circle of silver dancers, the flower stalks of a chalk lettuce *(Dudleya pulverulenta)* rise from the central rosette.

Early morning sunlight illuminates the pink veins and yellow throats of a cluster of Mexican evening primrose flowers.

Big as a peony, a vibrant pink and red orchid cactus flower dangles from fleshy, notched leaves.

A group of viper's bugloss flower spikes, studded with little blue stars, seems to march past a pine branch.

A Passageway Garden
Care-free plants fill a small, shady spot

A garden of shade-loving plants surrounding a brick path creates a pleasant interlude between the front yard and the backyard, visible beyond the gate. Delicate flowers highlight a lush carpet of contrasting foliage.

by Patricia Taylor

When people tell me they have too little space to grow flowers, I like to show them a tiny passageway garden next to the northeast corner of my house in Princeton, New Jersey. Here, over two dozen different perennials are tucked into a 9-ft. by 9½-ft. shaded area, yet from April through October, they produce a fine display of blossoms in pinks, blues, whites and yellows.

The garden is a gem, and I love it, particularly since it needs no more than two or three hours of maintenance per month. It has shown me that a small garden really can be better.

Besides requiring less effort, a small garden exhibits a charm not found in larger ones. Single specimens of many plants can be squeezed into one spot, much as is done in flower arranging. Cramming a diversity of plants into a small space creates a pleasing effect, while doing so in a larger space can result in a hodgepodge appearance.

My passageway garden came into being in 1988, as part of an effort to replant a part of the lawn that was torn up when my husband and I added a new room to our house. While it was a simple matter to repair most of the damage by spreading topsoil and sowing grass seed, one area presented a true challenge. It was a small, dark corner that would function solely as a way to get from the front to the backyard.

An old, 10-ft.-tall lilac bush at the edge of this area partially hindered passage. The lilac obviously needed to be pruned, and once we did so, it made a lovely foliage arch over the area. With this airy ceiling and a walled corner formed by the addition to our house, we realized we had the beginnings of a "garden room"— an enclosed, defined space waiting to be filled with plants.

Designing the garden
Our thinking was influenced by a recent trip to England, where we viewed the garden rooms created by Vita Sackville-West at Sissinghurst and Lawrence Johnston at Hidcote. Even more inspiring to me was the Oxford garden of Mrs. Anne Dexter. In a backyard measuring only 21 ft. by 70 ft., she has fashioned a stunning collection of beds

filled with herbaceous, alpine and shade-loving plants, tied together by a brick path that winds from one end of the garden to the other.

I had much less room than these gardeners, but their approach inspired me. These English gardens had brick walls or established shrubs surrounding them. To enclose our small shade garden, we settled for a 3-ft.-high lattice fence, which my husband built. One part of the fence skirts the property border, behind the lilac, and extends to the house with a gate leading into the backyard. We left the garden's front entrance unfenced, as an invitation to guests to enter the backyard.

Given the wretched condition of the clay soil, which had been packed down by workmen and machines, we made a path of dry-laid brick, rather than grass, through the garden. The dull red of the old brick contrasts nicely with the surrounding plants throughout the year.

We then turned our attention to the planting area abutting the house. Here, to add interest, we created a small, raised, brick-edged bed, which curves between the addition and the older part of the house. Beyond the corner of the house, the 1½-ft.-wide bed is at ground level, and so is a 3½-ft-wide bed on the other side of the path. Clearly, something had to be done to improve the packed clay soil next to the house.

Fortunately, we had a pile of well-rotted horse manure—the result of a perennials-for-manure barter with one of the carpenters who worked on the addition. To this we added bags of sand and peat moss, and dug in the mixture to a depth of at least 2 ft.

Acquiring plants

Now it was time to choose plants. In doing so, I had two important considerations. First, only shade-tolerant plants would do well here, as the raised bed at the corner of the house gets no sun at all and the remainder of the garden receives no more than four hours of sun per day. Of course, shade is a relative term. We have bright shade because of the reflection from white aluminum siding on the house.

Second, all the plants had to be tough, hardy perennials. I did not

Blue flowers of ajuga pop up through astilbe leaves. Above them are palm-shaped bloodroot leaves. These deeper greens are set off by the silvery leaves of Japanese painted fern (right).

The heart-shaped leaves of epimedium create a dramatic contrast with the finely-dissected leaves of pink bleeding heart.

want to be bothered with replanting annuals each year. In addition, I did not want to spend money for fertilizers or pesticides, nor did I want to spend time applying them or watering the garden.

Fortunately, some tried and true performers were already growing in the border farthest from the house, and I left some of them in place. Sensitive ferns (Onoclea sensibilis) and ajuga (Ajuga reptans) were scattered about, as well as two variegated hostas (Hosta undulata), a clump of yellow flag (Iris pseudacorus) and the lilac.

I cleaned out a lot of the ferns, told the ajuga to stay at the very front of the border and pared back the hosta to one small clump. In front of this border, I planted short plants with dramatically contrasting foliage. Most of them don't grow taller than 1 ft. They include fern-leaf corydalis (Corydalis cheilanthifolia), bugloss (Brunnera macrophylla), cuckoo flower (Cardamine pratensis), bloodroot (Sanguinaria canadensis) and Japanese painted fern (Athyrium niponicum pictum).

My plants came from other parts of my property, mail-order nurseries, and most important of all, from fellow gardeners as gifts or trades. I really feel that there is no other activity that so vividly demonstrates the generous nature of gardeners. We enjoy sharing our knowledge and our products to a degree unprecedented in any other endeavor.

The fern-leaf corydalis, for example, was a gift from a gardening friend, Helen Benedict. She knows how adamant I am about planting only easy-care perennials and assured me that it was a wonderful plant, one that thrives and spreads in sun or shade in her Rocky Hill, New Jersey, garden. True to its popular name, it looks like a fern most of the year. In spring, however, it sends up spikes covered with bright yellow flowers. Since this plant was not available in commercial trade, I never would have found it without Helen. (Winterthur Museum has a limited supply of Corydalis cheilanthifolia plants. For a free plant list, write to the Winterthur Museum, Attn: Garden Shop, Winterthur, DE 19735.)

Other friends contributed taller plants to join the yellow flag foliage toward the rear of the wider border. Barton Rouse, a gourmet chef at one of the Princeton University eating clubs, dug up the great bellflower (*Campanula latifolia*) and flowering raspberry (*Rubus odoratus*) from his garden. Had I been put off by the description of the great bellflower in *Wyman's Gardening Encyclopedia* as a "coarse-leaved perennial," I would have missed out on a lot of blue flowers in summer. The flowering raspberry is a wonderful, pink-flowered shrub native to the United States. Ironically, it's quite popular in Great Britain, but is almost unheard of in this country. This fruitless raspberry requires no staking.

My plant choices were dictated by flower color or foliage appearance. In the sunless, raised bed next to the house, for example, I planted hosta 'Blue Umbrellas' for the striking effect of its large, blue-green leaves. On either side of it, I put in bishop's hat (*Epimedium* × *rubrum*). This plant features dainty, pink-and-white flowers in the spring and light green, heart-shaped foliage, often tinged with red on its border.

At the edge of the bed, I planted pink-flowered bleeding heart (*Dicentra eximia*) and yellow corydalis (*Corydalis lutea*). These two plants both have delicate, blue-green foliage that contrasts nicely with the bold leaves of 'Blue Umbrellas' spreading above. Even more important, from a color point of view, are their long bloom periods, which begin in May. The flowers of the bleeding heart are open for at least three months, and those of the corydalis for six months.

The rest of this border is filled with the silver-gray-spotted leaves of lungwort (*Pulmonaria saccharata* 'Mrs. Moon'), hardy begonia (*Begonia grandis*), Jacob's ladder (*Polemonium reptans*), astilbe 'Deutchland', a small variegated hosta, foxgloves and more bloodroot.

The flowering season

Bloom in the garden starts in April with the brilliant white bloodroot flowers, the blue-and-pink lungwort flowers and the yellow fern-leaf corydalis. In May, the garden is truly lovely when the delicate blue flowers of Jacob's ladder, ajuga and bugloss join in with the pinks of the bleeding heart, bishop's hat, cuckoo flower and foxgloves. At the same time, the two corydalis species and American columbine (*Aquilegia canadensis*) add a dash of yellow.

Yellow-flowered corydalis, a long-blooming perennial, is flanked by epimedium (left, background), bleeding heart (left, foreground) and lungwort (right), with its silvery-gray-spotted leaves.

The delicate, blue flowers of bugloss, a May-blooming perennial, nestle beneath bold, variegated hosta leaves.

The focus of attention in the garden bounces back and forth between the borders. For example, during the month of June, the white plumes of the astilbe come out at the end of the border closest to the house, while the first of the deep pink blossoms of the flowering raspberry appear at the back of the wider border. In July, the pale blue flowers of the variegated hosta shoot up, and the deeper blue ones of the great bellflower appear on 3-ft.-tall spikes behind the green-and-white hosta leaves.

The bellflower and the corydalis continue to bloom throughout the month of August. Even more important at this hot, tired time of the garden year is the color contributed by foliage. The variegated hosta adds white; the lungwort, splashes of silver-gray; and the Japanese painted fern, a tinge of maroon on the midribs of its ghostly, greenish-white leaves.

In early September, the bellflower finally stops blooming, but the pink-and-white flowers of the hardy begonia soon appear. And the yellow of the corydalis keeps on until the end of October.

The garden is not a static one. Once the plantings began to fill in, I yanked out more ajuga and ferns and added two tiarellas, (*Tiarella wherryi* and *T. polyphylla*). The former plant is covered with puffy spikes of soft pink flowers in May and has warm green foliage that goes quite well with that of the ferns and the bloodroot. The latter is an exquisite Japanese native, with maroon veins highlighting its rounded, green leaves. Mine hasn't bloomed yet, but I'm eagerly awaiting the arrival of its white flowers.

Another garden friend, Mary Mills, has recently given me two very early spring-blooming plants—pink-flowered *Corydalis solida* and blue-flowered *Scilla tubergeniana*. When the leaves of both plants go dormant after bloom, the empty space is covered by the large, dark green foliage of the bugloss.

My garden, which is just three years old, has convinced me that a small space, even in a shaded area, can easily be transformed into an attractive and carefree arrangement. With no more effort than occasional deadheading and tidying up, I enjoy a lovely display throughout the growing season. □

Patricia Taylor is the author of Easy Care Perennials *and gardens in Princeton, New Jersey.*

Photos: Alison H. Speckman

Winding paths encourage visitors to explore this diverse and artfully arranged plant collection where the common and the unusual grow side-by-side. The garden is a shining example of an extensive collection, inspired by a love for plants and an unstoppable curiosity, that has been unified by artful design to make a cohesive garden. (Photo taken at A on site plan.)

A Collector's Garden

A passion for plants shapes a design

by Constance Hansen

As an incurable collector and compulsive gardener, I have always gardened wherever I happened to be. For many years, I gardened in central California, but I was always homesick for Oregon, where I'd lived as a child. My earliest memories of flowers are from there, and I remembered the way I could just walk outdoors and be surrounded by trees. I also wanted to live near the ocean. Finally, in 1973, I moved to coastal Oregon and bought the overgrown plot that is now my garden. When I saw its stream, swampy area and large shade trees, I knew I could make a home for Japanese iris, ferns, rhododendrons and many of my favorite plants. Roughly 150 ft. by 200 ft. on the end of a city block, the plot was an open meadow on the south, with the stream and the swampy area to the north. Two years ago, my property full of plants, I bought an adjacent ⅓ acre.

Shaping the garden

The layout of my garden followed a natural progression, based on the gentle contours of the land and the plants I wanted to grow. Two of my main considerations were where to make paths and how to achieve some feeling of privacy in a spot exposed to view on all sides. (See site plan on facing page.)

A visitor's first impression of the garden is from the driveway, where grass paths winding around island beds come into view and then lead on to a succession of beds and borders.

I never made an overall plan for the garden; I just did it. For example, I was intrigued for some time by a grassy area on the north edge of the meadow. Its gentle slope formed the shape of a comma, and it seemed like the ideal location for a large collection of rhododendrons and other plants that friends had given me. And so it became my "comma" bed. Most of my beds developed in this way, often inspired by gifts from gardening friends.

At first, it seemed as though the space here was endless. I planted with a free hand and allowed many natives to come up on their own. Over the years, as the plants, especially the rhododendrons, have grown larger, I've had to expand the beds and reduce the grassy areas between them to narrow paths. To the north of the stream, I did leave two open, grassy spots from which to enjoy the plantings.

Enclosing the garden has been an ongoing process. I think a fence is unfriendly, and a 700-ft. one would have taxed my limited finances and building ability. (I do all the garden work myself.) I still make a gesture toward fencing with bamboo canes. And the growth of shrubs and small trees is gradually creating a feeling of enclosure.

Favorite plant groups

Visitors often ask where I find so many different kinds of plants. The question reminds me of my early gardening days when I was full of wonder at all of the strange plants in other people's gardens. I try to explain that learning about plants takes time—reading books, studying catalogs, visiting gardens and nurseries and joining various specialist groups. The Oregon Hardy Plant Society has been a wonderful source of information for me.

In choosing plants for the garden, year-round interest is one of my goals. If I especially like a particular plant, I want to grow more than one. I like all flower colors, but when an occasional unfortunate color combination occurs, I either remove the offender, if doing so won't disturb the plants too much, or I try to look the other way while the plants are in bloom.

The plants I'm excited about range from the familiar to the less common. I'll describe some of my favorites here, but there are many others—heathers, euphorbias and viburnums, to name a few.

Rhododendrons and companions— Rhododendrons thrive in this mild maritime climate and in my slightly acidic soil. I now have over 300 species and cultivars. In the middle of the rhododendron season, the mass of flowers makes it hard to know where to look first. In a favorable year, they bloom from January to July.

Some writers dismiss rhododendrons as dull when they are out of bloom. These folks must be familiar

Most days of the year, the author can be found in the garden, a tool in one hand and her cart nearby. Here she tends iris and other water-loving plants in the swamp bed. Beyond, medium-height shrubs frame and unify the garden. (Photo taken at B on site plan.)

only with the large-leaved rhododendrons commonly used in foundation plantings, because, in fact, rhododendrons offer a wonderful variety of shapes, leaf forms and sizes, and flower colors. This genus includes forms that range from tiny-leaved ground-huggers to those that, over time, become large trees.

I have several favorite rhododendrons, most of them chosen for their handsome foliage. The undersides of the dark green leaves of 'Sir Charles Lemon' are covered with bright orange indumentum, or powder. The new growth of 'Bow Bells' is almost flame-like in color, while that of 'Whispering Rose' is a fine bronze. The dark green, shiny leaves of 'Golden Gate' form a neat, tidy bush; its flowers, a strange combination of orange with purple edges, are an added bonus. *Rhododendron callimorphum*, whose name means "beautiful form," has light green, shiny foliage and a fairly open growth habit, which I prefer over a dense growth habit in which shoots grow so closely together that one can't see the branches. I also like large rhododendrons such as 'Leonardslee Giles', a fast-grower with gigantic white flowers. For variety of form and bloom among the rhododendrons, I've planted occasional choice deciduous flowering shrubs and small trees, such as stewartias, viburnums, magnolias and Japanese maples.

In spite of the shade from the rhododendrons, a few low-growing plants are thriving. The wild iris (mostly forms of *Iris douglasiana, I. tenax* and *I. innominata*) have continued to do well. They seed all over the garden, acting in many spots as a ground cover and delighting me each spring with their new flower patterns and color combinations. Hostas also are filling in the vacant shady spaces.

Water-lovers—The swamp bed is wet until well into June. Here I grow many different moisture-loving iris (*Iris laevigata*, Japanese, Louisiana and Siberian iris). The latter bloom at the same time as the rhododendrons. A little farther along into the summer, queen-of-the-prairie (*Filipendula palmata*) produces feathery, pink flowers on 4-ft. to 5-ft. stems. Growing at the outer edge of

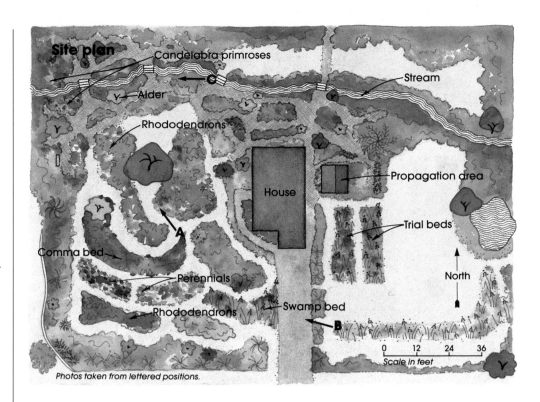

Site plan

Candelabra primroses

Alder

Stream

Rhododendrons

House

Propagation area

A

Comma bed

Perennials

Trial beds

Rhododendrons

Swamp bed

North

B

0   12   24   36
Scale in feet

Photos taken from lettered positions.

the bed are Michaelmas daisies, whose lavendar-to-purple fall blooms are a good companion to bronze sneezeweed (*Helenium autumnale*). Other plants that thrive in this wet soil are two white-flowered loose-strifes—*Lysimachia clethroides*, which runs around, and *L. ephemerum*, which stays in one place—and the tall, purple-flowered, native bulb, *Camassia leichtlinii*.

Primroses—In the shade of a huge alder near the stream are primroses and astilbes in a range of colors, together with many ferns, deciduous and evergreen azaleas, and rhododendrons. More water-loving iris grow in the few sunny spots here.

The candelabra primroses (*Primula japonica, P. pulverulenta* and others) display what I call Mexican colors—magenta, orange, yellow, raspberry and shades of purple to pink. They develop stalks up to 3 ft. tall and produce as many as seven clusters of flowers.

Other primroses that have given me a lot of pleasure are single and double forms of English primrose (*P. vulgaris*) and the 'Barnhaven' doubles, which come in many colors from pale cream through yellow, pink, rose and a rich red. Early in the spring, a dark-leaved viola (*Viola labradorica*) with little blue flowers makes a good companion in

color for the English primroses, although later in the season it overgrows them.

Hardy geraniums—The true hardy geraniums are among the perennials I like the best. There are many species, but I'll mention just a few. *Geranium sanguineum*, with magenta flowers, and a pink-flowered variety, 'Lancastriense', can fill bare spots with color all summer. *G. pratense* has large blue or white flowers and makes a clump about 18 in. tall. *G. macrorrhizum* forms a good, solid ground cover and has aromatic foliage, too. Flower color varies from pale pink to rose. My special favorite is *G. endressii*, whose pure pink flowers sit atop foot-high plants. One I acquired just last year is *G. psilostemon*, a 2-ft. to 3-ft. tall plant that bears brilliant magenta flowers with dark centers. *G. himalayense floraplena* is an interesting double-flowered plant, about 1 ft. high, with flowers of a mixture of lavender and rose. This is a fascinating genus; a collector is constantly tempted to acquire just one more.

Mixed 40s iris—These iris are not very well known, yet have given me great pleasure for the eight years or so that I have grown them. They are offspring of six species of

This native Douglas iris is one of the many herbaceous plants that form a carpet of seasonal color beneath taller shrubs and trees in the author's garden.

Aptly named, rhododendron 'Sir Charles Lemon' displays its golden leaves. The garden features rhododendrons of all kinds. They offer a surprisingly wide variety of sizes, shapes, textures and flower colors.

The punchy colors and large blooms of candelabra primroses highlight a shady border near the stream.

Sino-Siberian irises that hybridize readily among themselves and grow easily from seed to produce what are referred to as the "mixed 40s." (They have 40 chromosomes instead of 28 like Siberian irises.)

The variation in flower color of the "mixed 40s" seedlings is fascinating—from almost white through pale cream and ivory to very pale blue, blue-violet or deep red. Matching or contrasting shades are found within a single flower, and some flower parts are more deeply colored than others. Their bloom season comes just as the Siberian irises are finishing theirs.

The plants vary in height, some with flower stems under 2 ft. and others as tall as 4 ft., all arising from a slightly glaucous (bluish-gray) clump of foliage. The "mixed 40s" like the same moist conditions as do the Siberians, but may be a little less tolerant of drought. In my garden, they seem to be just as vigorous as the Siberians.

Care

This is not a low-maintenance garden. In fact, the subject of low-maintenance gardening leaves me sort of cold, as I believe it's for people who want to "furnish" the surroundings of their house as they do its interior, so it looks presentable and requires only sporadic attention, which can be provided by hired help. To those whose interests lie in the wonderful diversity of plants, and to those who have the time for their favorite occupation of caring for these plants, the topic of low maintenance has little charm.

Restraining the exuberant growth of the many wild plants such as sedges, horsetails or equisetums that enjoy the moist conditions here is a problem. But I'm following the admonition of Liberty Hyde Bailey in his small book, *The Garden Lover*. He says that if you can't get rid of a weed, learn to love it!

I feel I have achieved the desiderata expressed by the poet Abraham Cowley when he wished, "e'er he descended to the grave," for a small house with a large garden, a few friends and many books "both true, both wise and both delightful, too." To me, this place is a gardener's Shangri La.

Constance Hansen gardens in Lincoln City, Oregon.

Photo: Jerry Pavia

The red flowers of rhododendron 'Taurus' (right) and the pink ones of azalea 'Glamour' (left) brighten up a cool, green streamside planting. The open, grassy area beyond creates a sense of spaciousness within the garden. (Photo taken at C on site plan.)

A Formal Garden
Three simple principles create a cohesive design

This formal herb garden, composed of several roomlike areas, complements the architecture of the author's old farmhouse. The garden's geometric design is emphasized by snow, as shown here in the 18th-century-style garden "room." English dwarf boxwood plants, covered with burlap to protect them from cold-weather damage, sit alongside an arched trellis (left, background) that separates the formal and semiformal areas of the garden. (Photo taken at A on site plan, facing page.)

by Ragna Tischler Goddard

Visitors who walk through my formal herb gardens frequently comment that the orderly design conveys a sense of peace and balance. People who are accustomed to an informal garden with free-flowing naturalistic plantings and masses of flower color are often surprised by the appeal of a geometric, structured design such as mine. They're even more delighted when they find out that designing a formal garden is quite easy.

When my husband, Tom, and I first moved to Connecticut, we directed our attention to restoring our 18th-century farmhouse, with little thought of landscaping the surrounding yard. But as I gathered information to help us with the restoration, I soon realized that the house would be incomplete without a pleasing landscape to accompany it. I didn't want to be limited to the exact plantings of an historically accurate period garden, but I decided that a formal garden—one with a geometric arrangement of elements—would best complement the architecture of the house.

Designing a formal garden would also allow me to use my training in art and graphic design to good advantage. It fit my sense of aesthetics as well. When I first came from Germany to America 27 years ago, I was struck by the contrast between European gardens, which are seamlessly connected to an adjacent house, and American gardens, which often feature flower beds or a few rows of vegetables floating like islands on an endless lawn. Despite its creator's good intentions and hard work, a garden made up of disconnected elements such as these never really falls into place, while a connected one looks attractive from the start.

Few people realize how well suited a formal garden is for 20th-century living. Unless you've had the pleasure of tending one, you might imagine that it requires constant fussing and a battalion of full-time gardeners to maintain it. In fact, a formal garden needs less maintenance than, for example, an informal perennial garden of equal size. Having clearly defined walkways and beds makes it easier to control plants and weeds. Beds outlined by low-growing hedges appear well groomed even if there are weeds in the center.

I've slowly developed my garden over the past 19 years by following the principles that have shaped formal gardens since ancient times. Regardless of the size of your garden or the particular plants you want to grow, you can use these principles as a guide: 1) View the garden as an architectural element on your property. 2) Divide the garden into partially enclosed areas, or outdoor rooms, and link them with walkways, structures or plants. 3) Rely on foliage color, shape and texture for year-round interest.

The garden as architecture
From the beginning, I thought about the kind of garden I wanted to create, though I didn't draw up a detailed plan for it. With a definite idea to guide me, I

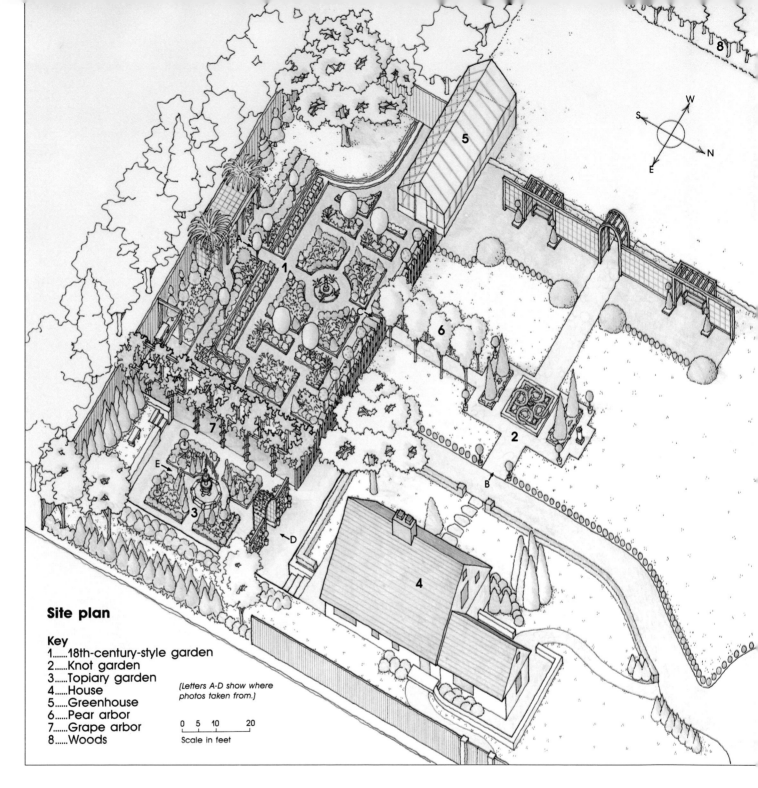

Site plan

Key
1......18th-century-style garden
2......Knot garden
3......Topiary garden
4......House
5......Greenhouse
6......Pear arbor
7......Grape arbor
8......Woods

(Letters A-D show where photos taken from.)

0 5 10   20
Scale in feet

could form the garden slowly, yet still have everything fit. As I sought ways to develop the garden, I researched garden history and found that many old concepts are as useful today as they were in times past.

My garden is modeled after a formal layout that can be traced back to the small domestic Sumerian gardens developed around 3000 B.C. in the region that is now southern Iraq between the Tigris and Euphrates Rivers. Interestingly enough, the Sumerian designs include some ideas we think of as modern, such as dividing a garden area into rooms.

The Sumerian gardens were composed of three essential elements: a house; an enclosure, such as a wall or fence that protected plants from harmful weather and excluded intruders; and a garden plot set within the enclosure. Both the garden and the enclosure were aligned with the house and became architectural elements. There was direct access from the house to the garden plot, which usually consisted of a square or rectangular piece of land. Two intersecting walkways, running north-south and east-west, divided the garden into four beds. This layout was referred to as the

fourfold garden. A cistern was often placed where the walkways met.

With these ideas in mind, all I had to do when I started my garden was to establish the north-south and east-west axes, both aligned with the house (see the site plan above). This gave me two lines of reference from which I could lay out square- or rectangular-shaped gardens. As a result, the entire yard has looked well planned from the start, yet there's always room to add new elements or to connect existing ones.

I find that the most attractive gardens are those designed from the house out-

The 18th-century-style garden—Foliage of different colors, shapes and textures predominates throughout the gardens. The garden room *above* is distinguished by brick-edged beds and paths, a pleasing contrast to the many shades of green. Silver mound artemisia and lamb's-ears circle the sundial, while golden sage and woolly thyme fill the planters. Within the neatly clipped, true English dwarf boxwood hedge edging the bed *below,* a mass planting of southernwood and a clump of magenta-flowered gayfeather add a touch of informality and spontaneity to the garden. Red-flowered hibiscus, trained as standards, brighten the bed bordering the fence.

ward, with the most formal areas closest to the house and the less formal areas farther away. For my landscape, I imagined three circles radiating outward from the middle of the house, each representing a different planting area. In the circle nearest to the house, I've planted formal gardens, where they're easiest to tend and most visible. In the middle, I've created a semiformal, parklike lawn. Farthest from the house, I've left an existing natural woodland undisturbed. Depending on the size of your yard, more or less area can be devoted to each circle. On a smaller site, formal plantings might occupy the entire yard, while on a larger one, much of the property could be left in its natural state.

Outdoor rooms

To date, I've developed three separate areas, or rooms, in my garden: an 18th-century-style garden, a knot garden and a topiary garden. Each of these styles lends itself to a simple, formal layout based on the fourfold pattern of the Sumerian gardens. Because of the regular shapes of these rooms, I could easily align them to create vistas from one to another. These styles emphasize foliage, rather than flowers, creating an attractive look year-round. Viewed from different windows of the house, they extend the interior of the house into the outdoors, so I never feel closed in, even during a long Connecticut winter.

The gardens are aligned with the

house, and are connected to each other and to the house by walkways, fences, arbors or trellises. Taken together, the center of each garden and the house sit on the corners of a square. Each garden has a definite boundary. Geometrically arranged garden beds divide the 18th-century-style and topiary gardens into four equal plots each, and the four corners of the knot garden are marked by potted myrtle and rosemary trained into standards.

To distinguish the gardens from each other, I've designed each with different building materials and plants and a distinctive object at the center. In the knot garden, intertwining, ribbonlike plantings fill a stone-edged bed, which is surrounded by stone walkways. An ornamental sculpture rests in the midst of the knot pattern. In the 18th-century-style garden, brick-edged walkways and beds create a pattern around a central sundial. In the topiary garden, sculptured plants with strong vertical lines predominate, along with gravel-covered paths, cement-edged beds, stone walls, and a fountain at the center. The knot garden is purely decorative, and meant to be viewed from without, while the other two gardens are roomlike enclosures, to be enjoyed from within. As different as these gardens appear, they all share the same conceptual origin in the formal Sumerian gardens.

The 18th-century-style garden—I developed this garden first, drawing inspiration for it from the designs of European gardens of the 1500s and 1600s, which found their way to America by the 1700s. Confronted with nothing but a field of weeds, a small lawn and a 100-year-old grape arbor, I decided to center the east-west axis of this garden on the arbor. (To visually link the 18th-century-style garden with the house, I later built the knot garden.) Had I picked a random spot for my first garden, I would have ended up with one of those floating islands, something I wanted to avoid. The arbor and a solid board fence enclose the 50-ft. by 100-ft. area on the south and east. A typical 18th-century picket fence bounds the north side, while one on the west side, still to be completed, allows an unobstructed view into the woods.

Once had I established the perimeter of the garden, I developed the area within. First I positioned raised beds, the sundial and arbor-covered benches. Several container-grown bay plants (*Laurus nobilis*) trained as standards serve as focal points. The careful positioning of these architectural elements contrasts with the flowing lines in the natural areas beyond the garden.

The brick-edged raised beds curve around the sundial in the center of the garden. The beds, along with an extensive drainage ditch, also greatly improve my poorly drained soil. Brick paths run

The knot garden—The closeup *above* shows, from front to back, the variety of low-growing herbs that compose the knot garden: gray-green woolly thyme at the edge of the bed, grasslike thrift, blue-green rue, deep-green germander, circle onion and silvery lamb's-ears.

The tapestry pattern of the knot garden *above* is clearly revealed when viewed from the west door of the house. Tall junipers dominate the nearby rectangular beds; a potted sweet bay (on the left) and a rosemary (on the right) mark one walkway. Since this photo was taken, the area beyond the garden has been developed to create a view into the distant woods, as shown *below*. (Photos taken at B on site plan.)

north-south and east-west across the garden and meet at the sundial.

While some of the plants in this garden are precisely shaped and symmetrically arranged, others are nestled together in a less formal manner. With a symmetrical layout to firmly establish the structure of the garden, I've been able to allow for a few surprises and still maintain an orderly look.

The knot garden—Our house is perched on a small rise 10 ft. above the rest of the yard and looks out on a flat area adjacent to the 18th-century-style garden. I needed something to fill that space, and a knot garden seemed the perfect solution. This style of planting, especially popular in the 15th and early 16th centuries in England, consists of interlacing patterns of low-growing, compact herbs with contrasting foliage, such as lavender, germander, santolina and rue, as well as boxwood. Originally designed for castle courtyards, knot gardens were meant to be viewed from above. Our house would become our castle from which to view this garden.

The knot garden proper is a 12-ft. by 12-ft. square. A stone walkway bordering the garden leads to the house and to the 18th-century-style garden. Setting off the knot garden are rectangular beds of germander, rue, silver-leaf veronica (*Veronica incana*), perennial flax (*Linum perenne*), silver-leaf horehound (*Marrubium incanum*), woolly thyme, thrift (*Armeria maritima*), clove pinks, 'Wichita Blue' junipers (*Juniperus scopuloram*) and potted herbs trained into standards.

The knot garden looks good in summer when the little hedgelike plants make a pattern of contrasting foliage colors, shapes and textures. It also looks nice in winter, when a heavy frost or a light dusting of snow delicately traces the pattern of the garden, emphasizing its architectural quality.

Over the walkway between the knot garden and the 18th-century-style garden, I made a pleached arbor from 'Seckel' pear trees. Pleaching is an ancient technique where branches are intertwined and grow into a solid canopy with no permanent support beneath. The branches of the trees create the actual arbor. It will be several years before the arbor is completed, and even then I'll need to continue trimming it to keep it shaped, but it's well worth the effort. The knot garden compels visitors to look downward, and the pear arbor draws their eyes upward. The flowering canopy is magical to walk beneath in spring, and provides welcome shade in summer.

The topiary garden—A topiary garden, which features boxwood plants trained into formal shapes, completes the square formed by the other two gardens and the house. A fountain at its center is

aligned with the sundial in the 18th-century-style garden.

More than any of the other gardens, this corner of the yard is an outdoor room in the truest sense of the word. One side is enclosed by the grape arbor, two more sides by stone retaining walls that my husband built, and the front of the garden by a rose-covered arched trellis. The walls give the illusion of a semi-sunken garden, making it an even more intimate space.

Pleasing proportions create a peaceful atmosphere in a garden. Here, as in the other gardens, I've thought carefully about how the sizes and shapes of the structures might affect the viewer. For example, the arch of the trellis measures one-half circle plus 1 in. This extra inch gives the impression that the arch is rising, adding lightness rather than weight to the structure.

Within the topiary garden, four concrete-edged beds surround a large fountain. For added texture and color, I've in-

Pleaching, an ancient training technique, was used to fashion this living arbor of pear trees over the walk between the 18th-century-style and knot gardens. (Taken at C on site plan.)

terspersed a variety of herbs with the boxwoods and planted junipers (*Juniperus virginiana* 'Burkii'). Your eye is drawn to a second, small fountain mounted on a wooden wall at the far end of the grape arbor. On a warm summer day, the sweet scent of the roses, the shade of the grape arbor, the drooping bunches of grapes and the soft trickle of the water invite guests to linger and rest on the benches beneath the stone walls or to walk through the garden.

I designed and constructed the large central fountain from an assortment of commercially available pieces. Water cascades from the top and from the four sides downward into an octagonal basin, and is recycled by two hidden pumps. Planter boxes filled with English ivy surround the fountain. As the vines trail over the outside of the boxes, I weave them into garlands. I must confess that having a fountain in Connecticut is a challenge, though I wouldn't want to do without one. Every year I need to drain it and to re-

seal the cracks caused by temperature changes and frost heaves.

Foliage for year-round interest

My gardens include a wide variety of plants, but I've concentrated on those whose foliage color, shape, texture or fragrance contributes to the garden throughout the year. Ground covers and plants for edging the beds make up the bulk of the plantings. As accents, I've included plants with particularly intriguing foliage color or texture or colorful flowers. Many of the plants I grow are those I learned to love as a child, such as chamomile, tansy, sweet woodruff and cornflowers, while others are newer additions to my palette.

For ground covers in the sun, I've planted lemon- and caraway-scented thyme and woolly thyme (*Thymus* 'Doone Valley', *T. Herba-barona* and *T. pseudolanuginosus*). In sun or semi-shade, several varieties of bugleweed (*Ajuga reptans*), including some with variegated leaves, and different species of speedwell (*Veronica* spp.) carpet the ground.

To edge the beds, I use dwarf English boxwood (*Buxus sempervirens* 'Suffruticosa'), which requires winter protection in my climate (USDA Zone 6). Spraying established plants with Wilt-Pruf, an antidesiccant, protects them adequately. I spray in late fall before temperatures drop below 45°F. Newly planted boxwoods must be wrapped with burlap to ensure survival through their first winter. For edging the beds, I also use germander, winter savory, rue, hyssop, santolina and lavender, to name a few. These plants form little hedges, varying in height from 1 ft. to 2 ft. tall, depending on how hard I trim them. With foliage color ranging from deep green to blue-green to gray, this group of plants offers me much opportunity to make pleasing patterns.

For accents, I particularly like to include tall plants such as elecampane (*Inula Helenium*) and angelica, and those with striking foliage color—the variegated gold or purple-flecked sage varieties, or silver-foliage plants such as lamb's-ears (*Stachys byzantine*). Some other favorites are the rich green foliage of fernleaf tansy (*Tanacetum vulgare* var. *crispum*) and the lacy-textured leaves of artemisia. Colorful flowers, such as red, pink or yellow yarrow (*Achillea* spp.), red valerian (*Centranthus ruber*) and purplish-pink wood betony (*Stachys officinalis*), stand out against the grays and greens of the rest of the garden. □

Ragna Tischler Goddard gardens at the Sundial Herb Garden in Higganum, Connecticut. The garden is open to the public free of charge weekends from 10 a.m. to 5 p.m. Call 203-345-4290 for directions.

Photos, above and facing page: Staff

The topiary garden—A rose-covered trellis *above* invites visitors to enter the topiary garden, where they can stroll among formally trained boxwood plants and enjoy the sound of water in the fountain. The arch is designed to give the impression that it is rising upward, adding lightness to the structure. The containers at the outer corners of the trellis contain myrtle; those at the base of the archway hold olive trees. The fountain *below,* which author Goddard built from commercially available components, helps create a peaceful atmosphere in the topiary garden. (Photos taken at D and E on site plan.)

Hillside Refuge

A small, intimate garden, forty years in the making

by Mark Kane

Gardening stole up on Sylvia Davidson. She had a demanding job—assistant to a movie executive—with problems that preoccupied her at work and at home. "I wasn't really a gardener," she says, "I just pulled weeds. One weekend, I was weeding and thinking about an especially difficult problem, when I had the strangest sensation that all my troubles were being absorbed by the earth. They seemed to leave through my hands as I pulled up weeds. The next weekend, I tried it again, and it worked again—it was accidental therapy. And that's how I started. From then on, gardening became my other life."

A lifelong garden intimately reflects the taste and character of the gardener. Davidson bought her house in the early 40s, became a gardener ten years later, and has gardened on the same small property ever since. When she invited me to visit, I felt privileged.

My first glimpse of the garden was surprising. Davidson lives on a narrow, crowded street in the foothills of Los Angeles. The driveway, just long enough for one car, fills most of the front yard. When I rang the

Blooming rhododendrons and azaleas flank the narrow entrance to a maze of paths in the hillside portion of a 40-year-old city garden. Small but private, the garden is the owner's refuge. (Photo taken at A on site plan.)

doorbell, I wondered if the backyard would be just as small and exposed. Davidson opened the door, welcomed me to her home, and led me to the living room at the back of the house, where floor-to-ceiling windows looked out onto a shady patio and the garden beyond. I saw a deep, narrow vista with mixed borders on each side, a meandering sweep of lawn between them, and a steep hillside at the back, bright with rhododendrons and azaleas in flower. The backyard was only 95 ft. wide and 150 ft. deep, yet no neighboring roofline intruded on the view. In spite of the city that had grown up around it, the garden was a refuge, completely private, enclosed by walls of bloom and greenery.

The appeal of the garden

Two features distinguish Davidson's garden. One is maturity—the dignity and steadfast character bestowed by trees planted 50 years ago and vines as thick as hawsers. The other is intimacy, created by a sunken patio and an artful design that encloses a small lot with a variety of perennials, shrubs and trees.

The patio, sheltered by a tall lath arbor, is uncommonly inviting and pleasant. When Davidson started the garden, she hired a landscape architect who recontoured the sloping backyard into level terraces near the house. She devoted the first terrace to the patio and the next to the lawn and mixed borders. The main attraction of the patio is its placement 2½ ft. below the garden. When you look out from the patio, the garden encloses the view in a way that makes the backyard feel private, like another room of the house.

Stepping onto the patio, you view the garden from an unusual angle. The lawn and mixed borders are foreshortened, like the highway seen from a car, an effect that lends the garden depth. The illusion is reinforced by the lawn curving out of sight, narrowing as it recedes.

Two Japanese plums, one in each border, pinch the lawn into a waist midway to the back of the terrace. Neighboring houses, less than 30 ft. away from the patio, are screened by plants. When you stand on the patio, shrubs and perennials in the garden rise to eye level, while apples, apricots and the Japanese plums stand well overhead, blocking the view left and right.

When you sit on the patio, the view changes dramatically. The lawn

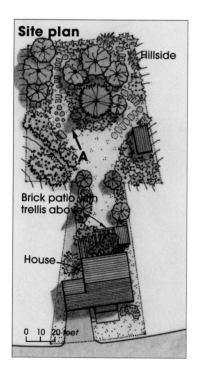

Site plan

Hillside

A

Brick patio with trellis above

House

0 10 20 feet

rises out of sight and the mixed borders reach overhead, blending into the hillside beyond. A concrete retaining wall runs the length of the patio, its top just higher than the soil on the other side. The flowers along the top of the wall stand at eye level, underlining the view like window boxes. The arbor's square posts and timber joists, darkened by shade, transform the bright garden beyond into a framed tableau. At one corner of the patio, the ropy stems of an old wisteria twine up a post, and a canopy of

Illustration: Vince Babak

An exotic combination of plants brightens the front of a border. A trailing geranium with bright red flowers weaves among the green blades of irises. The rosette of pale, fleshy leaves in the foreground is a hybrid echeveria called 'After Glow', not hardy outdoors in cold regions but a striking potted plant indoors. The dark, fleshy leaves flecked with water spots belong to a shrubby succulent from Morocco, *Aeonium arboreum* 'Schwartzkopf'.

Glowing in the sun, the 5-in. flower of a South African protea resembles a burst of fireworks.

Twisting steps lead up the hillside to a path that runs across the slope. Inexpensive and durable, the steps and path are made of planks on edge, held in place by lengths of galvanized steel water pipe driven deep into the ground (their tops are just visible as small circles against the planks).

shade plants. Like a ceremonial door, the entrance to the garden leads between two posts and up a set of steps through the retaining wall.

The love of plants

Davidson has followed her own inclinations in garden design and choice of plants. The mixed borders, lawn and hillside are the main elements of the garden's design, but they've changed repeatedly over the years, in part because Davidson cares for plants by listening to them. "They talk to me," she says. "They tell me they're thirsty, they need feeding, or they need to be moved. I moved the daisies five times before they found a home."

She has tried many plants over the years, gifts from friends, plants that caught her eye in a nursery, plants she brought back from her travels. "If I liked it, I tried it," she says. For a visitor from the Northeast, some of the plants were rare treats, among them proteas, South African shrubs with flowers that look like fireworks (see the photo at upper left); a bottlebrush tree covered with bright red, bushy flowers; and a bristly, exotic pine, the podocarpus. I also saw a mystery plant. It was a gift, and all Davidson knew was that the name might be 'Schwartzkopf.' It looked unearthly. About 4 ft. tall, 'Schwartzkopf' has a few leafless, fleshy branches tipped with rosettes of near-black leaves (visible in the photo on p. 49). I learned later that it's a cultivar of a Moroccan succulent, *Aeonium arboreum*, that comes to us via Holland.

The mixed borders flower profusely. There are azaleas and rhododendrons, cinerarias, gerbera daisies, geraniums, phlox, violets and many others. In an angle between the house and the end of the patio,

wisteria leaves covers the end of the arbor. An enormous bougainvillea in full flower spreads across the opposite half of the arbor, spilling over the edge in streamers to frame the view of the garden like bunting. Stray stems hang through the lath, glowing with bright pink flowers.

Sitting on the patio, with cool bricks underfoot, shaded by the arbor, you are in a garden room. Flowers and shrubs screen one end of the patio, and a tool shed covered with ivy closes the other end. Behind you, the wall of the house is a mural painted in swirling ribbons and islands of pale and dark green— an abstract garden. In front of you, the verdant hillside fills the view completely. Potted plants rest on the brick floor around the edge of the patio, bringing flowers within arm's reach, and a bookshelf against the house holds a "library" of potted

An Australian bottlebrush tree covers itself with distinctive, bright red flowers. The pale green leaves below belong to a giant fern.

Davidson grows orchids as ground covers. They fill the nook with strap-like leaves, arching stems and gleaming, exotic flowers.

Davidson's overflowing garden led to the creation of a charity to benefit a school for children with learning disabilities. "The school had financial difficulties," she says, "and one night I got the idea of selling plants to raise money. Seedlings came up all over my garden by the thousands. We just pulled them up and threw them away. So I thought we could pot them instead and sell the plants. We'd make arrangements with a bank and set up our display outside on paydays. In five years, we raised $20,000. We kept the school going until the state started helping the children."

A secret world on the hillside

Davidson has transformed the steep hillside into a garden. When she bought her home, the hillside held a dead pear orchard, a few trees and poison oak. She saved four small oaks and a pine, cleared the rest of the slope piecemeal and planted flowering shrubs, tree ferns, calla lilies, birds of paradise, hydrangeas, cinerarias and more pines. The soil is decomposed granite, basically crumbs of rock, but plants grow well with regular watering. Sprinklers on 6-ft. risers are concealed among the shrubs. The oaks are now 30 ft. tall, and a pine that Davidson planted high up the slope is 60 ft. tall. The trees have changed the character of the garden. Once sunny, it is now largely shaded.

Hidden among the shrubs and trees on the hillside is a maze of paths and steps. Davidson and her housekeeper gardened at first without them. "We were like goats," she says.

But finally she hired help and made paths that lead to every part of the slope. The paths and steps are narrow dirt terraces, held in place by planks and stakes made from galvanized steel water pipe (see the photo at left). The construction is simple, inexpensive and sturdy. From the patio and garden, the paths are invisible, a hidden treat. When I explored them, I found myself in a secret world. Barely 2 ft. wide, the paths and steps are walled by foliage. Calla lilies lean white trumpets across the paths, and the bristly, red flowers of the bottlebrush tree

Inviting and cool, the patio lies two steps down from the garden, under a 10-ft. tall lath arbor half-covered with bougainvillea. The patio's low placement makes the garden feel intimate, like another room of the house.

hang at eye level. As I walked, I could rarely see more than 10 ft. ahead, so every turn brought surprises— a confluence of paths, a bird of paradise plant with its spiky flower the shape of a cockatoo's crest, a big pine with its gray plates of bark. Hidden birds sang, and the city all around seemed to disappear. I might have been in a state park, but I was barely 100 ft. from the house.

The rewards of lifelong gardening

One of the great pleasures of gardening is endless variety. You can fall in love with daylilies and never exhaust the choices. Then, if your ardor cools and daylilies become just another wonderful plant, you can take up azaleas, veronicas, violets or any of a thousand other irresistible plants. Davidson has a rich and full garden, and a lifetime of gardening behind her, but she still acquires new passions. Lately, she's taken up roses and gerbera daisies. The daisies spill all over the garden, contributing accents of bold color in a wide range of hues— yellow, orange, red. Her small collection of roses stands alone, with big flowers perfuming the air. "I just love them," she says. "I really didn't know if I could grow them, but they seem to like it here. They give me so much pleasure."

Gardening on the same property for decades offers respite from constant change. When Davidson bought her home in the early 40s, her parents worried about her moving so far from town. The street was paved with gravel and had no lights. Now houses crowd the street, and around the corner, just two miles away, is Rodeo Drive and the center of Beverly Hills. The city grew around her, rising up the canyon and over the hills, but the garden preserves the quiet and privacy of another era.

Though Davidson no longer cares for the garden herself, it remains her refuge and solace. "The garden's gotten beyond me," she says. "I'm too old to take care of it." She hires help, but still listens to what the plants are saying. "I go up the hill every two weeks or so. You have to. It's the only way to see how things are doing." Why does she still climb those twisting steps? "I take care of the garden," she says, "and the garden takes care of me." □

Mark Kane is executive editor of Fine Gardening.

Rocky Mountain Garden

An Englishman's touch at 7400 ft.

by Andrew Pierce

Eleven years ago, my wife and I moved to the mountain community of Evergreen, Colorado. Anxious to get away from the hustle-bustle of life on the flatlands near Denver, we wanted the feeling of living up in the Rockies. We found a 0.6-acre lot with a spectacular view, and had our house built so that from the breakfast table we can see 14,000-ft.-tall Mount Evans in its early-morning glory.

When we chose this site, I wasn't thinking about how I'd tackle gardening here. Practical concerns came first: hookups to city water and sewer services, a natural gas line, and a driveway that's not too steep for winter access. Even before we moved in, though, I began to assess the soil, slope, exposure and climate, and started moving rocks around. I've been working with plants all my life (first in England, then in Bermuda, and now in the States), and I can't resist the opportunity to create a new garden.

My garden in Evergreen is located at a 7400-ft. elevation, on a west-facing site with a 25° slope. The whole site is composed of large, sometimes broken, granite boulders interspersed with relatively shallow pockets of sandy, acid forest soil that's very low in nutrients. Normal precipitation here is about 20 in., spread throughout the year. Over half of this may come as snow—as much as 9 ft. to 13 ft. in a winter, sometimes covering the ground from mid-November to early April. Temperatures range from winter lows of -35°F to summer highs of perhaps 95°F, with a 70- to 90-day frost-free season in June, July and August.

Because of these factors—the high elevation and steep slope, shallow soil and rocky terrain, dry summers and snowy winters, extreme temperatures and a short growing season—most people in Evergreen don't even try to have a garden. Yes, perhaps, the situation limits what can be grown, but I don't look at it that way. Instead, I've relished the opportunity to explore a new setting, shape it into a landscape and fill it with plants I enjoy. I'll tell how I've dealt with the challenges as I lead you through a tour of the garden.

My garden wraps all around the house, and tapers off into the wild grasses, flowers and shrubs that grow in the shade of mature ponderosa pine and Douglas fir trees. Blending the garden into the natural scenery is important to me. The most intensively planted and maintained areas are closest to the house. Between these areas and the surrounding forest, there are transition zones where I've enriched the native vegetation by planting wildflowers, shrubs and trees that don't need watering or special care. Beyond that, the rest of the property is undeveloped.

In laying out the garden, I was guided by the nature of the site and the needs of different plants (see the site plan, p. 54). Basically, I worked around the rocks and trees I couldn't move, and positioned plants where they'd get the light, moisture and soil they needed. A steep rocky bank east of the house offered the right topography, drainage and exposure for a rock garden. Where the lower floor of the house opens out on the west, I made a level lawn where we can sit and enjoy the view. By keeping the lawn small, I could fit a colorful flower border along its edge. A vegetable patch is located in a sunny spot nearby, which I leveled as much as possible and filled with enriched soil. Plants that require moist soil and cool shade grow in a narrow bed along the north wall of the house, and the warm south wall makes a backdrop for a border of sun-loving perennials.

During construction, the contractor had to blast two or three very large boulders (in the 5- to 12-ton range) out of the garage site. He was quite ready to give those boulders another little shot and cart off the debris, but I persuaded him to move them around to the south side of the house, where they serve as corner points in the garden design. With these initial large boulders in place, I started to shape the rest of the garden.

This took the better part of three growing seasons, because I did all the work myself. Using pieces of local granite to lay dry stone walls, I created planting beds. The stones are rather randomly laid, but the walls are strong enough to hold the soil I've filled in behind.

Railroad ties make good steps for the pathways that wander through the garden. To integrate the steps into the garden and the rocky slope, I grouped a few risers at the ends of longer ramps, avoiding the appearance of a whole staircase of steps. Ties alone are too narrow to walk on comfortably, so I filled a 4-in. space behind each tie with good soil, and planted creepers such as thyme and woolly veronica (*Veronica pectinata*) to soften the appearance.

The native soil here is very sandy and extremely well-drained underneath a thin layer of pine-needle mulch. It was obvious from the start that I needed to build up the soil before I could begin to plant a garden. For example, to make a vegetable patch about 25 ft. by 30 ft., I made a retaining wall of heavy boards at the lower end, excavated a foot or so at the upper end and leveled the soil in between. After forking through the area to a depth of 12 in. and removing all the rocks, I was left with 6 in. to 8 in. of fine broken granite and sand. To this I added 4 in. of leaves (from Denver's fall throwaways), along with 4 in. of well-rotted stable cleanings (free from the local dump). Two or three more forkings and the actions of winter frost worked the mixture into reasonable soil by the next spring.

In the other parts of the garden, I followed a similar approach to soil improvement, although underlying rocks sometimes prevented cultivating down to 12 in. The slope was often too steep for a wheelbarrow, and I had to move rocks, soil and organic matter in buckets.

The rock garden covers about 400 sq. ft. on an uphill slope east of the house. This garden started out as a jumble of rocks that had rolled down the slope in a bygone era. Most were too large to relocate, but I repositioned a few of the smaller ones. The books say you should take care to align the rock strata in your garden to resemble that of the surrounding

Working around the granite boulders and mature conifers on his site, author Pierce has shaped a garden that's colorful throughout the short growing season. This view (looking downslope to the west) shows the sunny perennial border next to the south wall of the house. Pink-flowered sedum and malva, tall yellow goldenrod, and violet veronica are showy in late summer. (Taken at A on site plan, p. 54.)

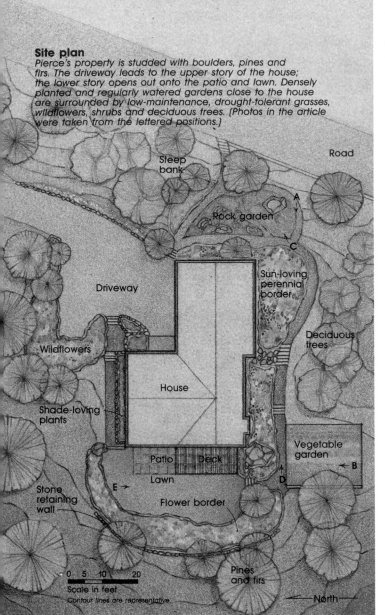

Site plan

Pierce's property is studded with boulders, pines and firs. The driveway leads to the upper story of the house; the lower story opens out onto the patio and lawn. Densely planted and regularly watered gardens close to the house are surrounded by low-maintenance, drought-tolerant grasses, wildflowers, shrubs and deciduous trees. (Photos in the article were taken from the lettered positions.)

Steep bank

Road

Rock garden

A

C

Driveway

Sun-loving perennial border

Deciduous trees

Wildflowers

House

Shade-loving plants

Vegetable garden

B

Patio   Deck

E →

Lawn

D

Stone retaining wall

Flower border

0 5 10   20
Scale in feet
Contour lines are representative.

Pines and firs

← North →

To create a 750-sq.-ft. vegetable garden, Pierce first built a wooden retaining wall and leveled the area behind it. Then he added generous amounts of autumn leaves and stable cleanings to build up the thin layer of sandy soil. (Taken at B on site plan.)

terrain, but I found that weathered granite covered in lichens looks good whichever way it lies. The abundance of rocks made an ideal setting for a rock garden, but in some places the native soil was only an inch or two deep. In order to create beds for planting, I had to work together the broken pieces of granite and then add small amounts of organic matter or already improved soil from other parts of the property for the soil mix.

With the slow growth rate of some of the plants, the rock garden is just beginning to look mature after seven years. At the top is a native juniper (*Juniperus communis*), possibly 200 years old, that's about 15 ft. across and 2 ft. tall. The lower edge of the garden blends into the native landscape, which I enhanced with a clump of aspen trees (*Populus tremuloides*). In between, native shrubs such as mountain mahogany (*Cercocarpus ledifolius*) and exotics such as broom (*Cytisus × kewensis*) and daphne (*Daphne × Burkwoodii*) add height and color when they bloom

in late May and early June.

Smaller plants—about 140 species of bulbs, succulents and herbaceous perennials—comprise most of the rock garden. Many are tiny gems, growing only a few inches tall or wide, but I treasure them for their growth form, foliage color or beautiful flowers. Some of the plants are rare or unusual ones that I've obtained through sales and swaps organized by the local chapter of the American Rock Garden Society, or at the annual spring plant sale hosted by the Denver Botanic Gardens. Some are natives, which I've propagated by collecting a few seeds or making cuttings of special plants I see when I'm out on a hike. (I never collect plants by digging them up, and I'm careful to respect the endangered species and leave them untouched.)

I enjoy the challenge of plants that are notoriously difficult to grow. Sometimes the so-called problems of my situation turn into advantages. For example, I've found that I can grow lewisias, which require excellent drainage, in the cracks of

a northwest-facing retaining wall near the rock garden. In nature, these thick-rooted, succulent-leaved plants grow only in partly shaded crevices in the higher mountains. My favorite is *Lewisia Tweedyi*—its glossy flowers open over a period of several weeks in spring.

Daphne 'Somerset' is another surprising success. I had to try planting one, because I love the intensely sweet fragrance of its pinkish-white flowers, but I expected it to be killed by our winter lows of -35°F. Instead, it survived, protected under a snowbank for months at a time. The snow flattens the branches, but it insulates them from the worst of the winter cold.

Rock-garden plants require soil that drains quickly after a rain or watering, but they can't tolerate prolonged dryness. I usually have to water the rock garden twice a week during the summer. In early May I divide, replant and rearrange plants in the rock garden. Other than that, the only maintenance needed is pulling a few weeds now and then, and removing

Illustration: Laura B. Goodwin

The rock garden is especially lovely in late May, when phlox 'Milstream Jupiter' (foreground) and the shrubs daphne and broom (center and back) are in full bloom. (Taken at C on site plan.)

Growing wild in rocky nooks and crannies at high altitudes in the West, lewisia flowers on a northwest-facing rock wall in Pierce's garden. Difficult to grow in cultivation, this plant forms a thick taproot and a rosette of crisp, succulent leaves.

Lichen-covered boulders and rocks on the site made a natural setting for a rock garden. These hen-and-chickens (*Sempervivum tectorum*) cling directly to the rocks and invite a close look at the details of the garden.

faded blossoms (unless I'm saving seeds to distribute to other rock gardeners).

The lawn is our outdoor living area. With rugged slopes all around, it's nice to have a flat place for relaxation. My little patch of green, approximately 10 ft. by 30 ft., is not a lawn by most people's standards—it's just a pocket handkerchief. But it's large enough for two chaise lounges and two whiskey and gingers, or even for entertaining a small group of friends. Keeping it modest fits my philosophy. I don't want my garden to be a burden—I just want to enjoy it. I wouldn't want to be tied down by too much mowing and other drudgery. We like to be free to enjoy the mountain scenery in the summer.

Creating a level area, even one this small, was quite a chore. I pulled rocks off to the side and brought in bucketfuls of soil from other parts of the lot. Later I built a rock retaining wall around the west (downhill) and north sides of the lawn, and expanded the area to include a flower border approximately 8 ft. to 10 ft. wide (see photo, p. 57).

I seeded the lawn with an "Alpine mix" from the local hardware store. It contains some Kentucky bluegrass, some fescues, a little ryegrass and a very small portion of clover. Clumps of perennials such as *Bergenia cordifolia*, with its broad shiny leaves, and the variegated ornamental grass *Miscanthus sinensis* are mainstays of the border. My favorite tulip, *Tulipa tarda*, with its white-tipped yellow flowers, blooms in front of the border for as long as five weeks in the spring. I'm quick to plant annuals such as petunias and snapdragons between the fading tulips, to supply color for the rest of the season.

Keeping the lawn lush and green and the flowers fresh and colorful requires irrigation in this dry climate. Our summer precipitation comes in heavy showers, rarely as gentle, all-day rains. Since summer rains may be weeks apart, I water every two or three days in between. An underground sprinkler system is out of the question on such a rocky site. Instead, I use oscillating sprinklers to cover the lawn and most of the garden areas, and I water the dry corners and those areas needing a bit more moisture with a hose. Watering is a time-consuming but satisfying activity. While I water, I carry a pair of light pruners to do some deadheading, and stop to pull out the occasional weed (my made-up soil is not a weedy one). It's a good time to relax and look at my plants.

Because the frost-free season is so short, I have to think carefully about what to plant in the vegetable garden. Tender crops such as tomatoes or peppers seldom reach maturity here; neither do corn, squash or cucumbers. I buy these fresh in the local supermarkets or get freebies from gardening friends. Beans and peas, however, are definitely included. I must have a row of English scarlet runner beans. The vines grow vigorously, the flowers attract hummingbirds, and the beans are tender and tasty. Sugar snap peas fruit all summer with our cool nights. I always plant a row of potatoes. The vines don't have time to mature and brown off—they're still green when the fall frost comes—but it's the tender "new" potatoes that have the best flavor. Little 'Bibb' lettuce, spinach and radishes grow fast even in cool weather, and make good crops for the salad basket. Leeks and carrots are hardy into the fall. I harvest them as late as October and store any extras in buckets of sand in the garage.

Each year I add more leaves, compost, and charcoal-studded ashes from the fireplace, so the soil in the vegetable patch is now the darkest in my garden and the first to warm up in the spring. This helps seeds, especially beans, germinate and get growing. Also, I've pruned the lowest branches off nearby surrounding trees in order to speed the flow of cold air down the slope, so that the garden doesn't sit in a "frost pocket."

Even so, in all but one of the past ten years there's been frost as late as June 5 or June 10—hard enough to kill bean or potato sprouts, if I had put them in earlier. At the other end, I've seen a killing frost as early as August 17 or August 23. When I'm choosing varieties of tender vegetables, the first information I look for in the catalog is the number of days to maturity. A span of 50 to 60 days is best, as July is the only month that's safely frost-free—so far. In an exceptional year such as 1987, we didn't see a frost from May 11 until almost the end of September, but I never plan on that.

During the frost-free season, plants grow fast in the bright mountain sunlight. In July, I've seen English beans grow 2 ft. or more a week. I run the rows of vegetables directly north and south, so that all of the plants receive some sun every day and none are shaded by rows of taller plants. (Also, since the garden slopes down to the west, this orientation means I'm irrigating in almost level channels between the rows, where water is easily retained.)

Along the north and south walls of the house, I've planted flowers. Taking advantage of the different exposures, there's a narrow bed for plants that appreciate cool, shady conditions on the north, and a sun-warmed border on the south. The difference is important, and plants definitely perform better when they're in the right place. The south border begins to warm up and dry out enough to need watering in mid-April, but the soil in the shady bed on the north is still icy then. Plants in the south border are exposed to greater extremes of temperature in both summer and winter.

The raised bed along the north wall of the house, about knee-high and 2½ ft. wide, is ideal for raising primulas. My first cowslips (*Primula veris*) bloom in June,

Stepping downhill along the south side of the house is a border filled with perennials that have proven hardy to the winter cold. June-blooming irises are followed by yellow goldenrod, white feverfew, pink sedum and purple veronica. (Taken at D on site plan.)

with clusters of clear-yellow or bronzy-colored flowers that hang neatly from the top of 6-in.- to 9-in.-tall stalks. The foliage stays green and fresh all summer. I usually divide the plants in the spring just as new growth starts, and often find plenty of self-sown seedlings to play with. In that bed I also grow the oh-so-difficult-for-Colorado, immensely beautiful, blue Himalayan poppy (*Meconopsis betonicifolia*). I can manage to get it to flower at my elevation, whereas down in Denver it never does. One reason is that the temperatures up here average 10°F lower, day and night, year round. Another is the winter protection the plants get from the layer of snow.

Along the south wall of the house, where the builder positioned the large boulders, I've fashioned a sunny perennial border about 50 ft. long by 5 ft. to 15 ft. wide. The border is edged by a path that slopes and steps from the rock garden above to the vegetable garden and lawn at the bottom. A few dozen specimen-size clumps are the backbone of the border, and groups of smaller plants fill in between. I don't strive to create perfect combinations of color and texture, as some gardeners do, but try to arrange the plants so that there are patches of bloom throughout the whole area over the entire season.

It's not hard to find sun-loving perennials to bloom in spring or in summer. The big problem is the early frost date in fall. For example, hardy chrysanthemums, he-

leniums and Japanese anemones will make it through the winters here, and grow well through the summer. They may even set buds, but inevitably they're damaged by frost before they flower, so I've given them up.

A different problem is that some plants flower abundantly here, but the blooms are ephemeral in our low humidity and intense hot sun. My irises make quite a show when they open, but individual blossoms wilt and fade after just three or four days. Daylilies are gone in less than a day. The thinner and more delicate the petals, the sooner a flower will wither away. There's nothing to do but enjoy them while they last. Colorado has only ten days a year without any sun, so bright skies and dry air are the norm—unlike my native England, where cool, damp, cloudy weather keeps flowers looking fresh for weeks.

Some of the perennials that make a lasting show of flowers in sunny July and August are *Veronica longifolia* 'Glacier Lake', with spikes of blue flowers; *Malva Alcea* var. *fastigiata*, with pink hollyhock-like blossoms; and *Sedum spectabile* 'Indian Chief', with rosy-pink flower clusters atop succulent foliage. The red flowers of Maltese-cross (*Lychnis chalcedonica*) look nice with the white flower clusters of feverfew (*Chrysanthemum Parthenium*). Sometimes I add annuals for summer color, if there's space to tuck them in front of the spring-blooming irises, for example.

The Indian summer that occurs after the first frost of autumn is more glorious if I can protect the summer-flowering annuals from being killed. These early frosts may appear for only a few nights before the temperatures go above freezing again. So I protect the best plants by laying dropcloths, sheets of plastic, or other coverings over them on these few frosty nights to prolong their welcome splash of color.

Finally frost comes to stay and the gardening season draws to a finish. I cut the perennial stalks down to 3-in. stubs and pull out the annuals. After the ground has frozen, I may apply a winter mulch, a layer of coarse organic matter such as oak leaves or pine needles. This insulates the soil and prevents the repeated freezing and thawing that can upheave plants. For nearly half the year, the garden lies dormant under a blanket of snow. Maybe that's why I enjoy it so much during the summer. □

Andrew Pierce is assistant director of the Denver Botanic Gardens.

Soaring to a high canopy, sweet gums shade a naturalistic garden inspired by the surrounding south Louisiana native landscape. Planted with small trees, shrubs, and low perennials, the garden has an open character at eye level that reveals the depth of the property. (Photo taken at A on site plan.)

In a Green Cathedral

Gardening for mystery and surprise in a wooded setting

by Wayne Womack

When Jon Emerson and I first saw the property that we've gardened on since 1977, we were struck with awe. The lot was 100 ft. by 400 ft., neglected, overgrown, and half-wild. Most prospective homebuyers, I suppose, would have been practical and turned away from the spot immediately, but we were captivated. I remember standing under a solid, towering canopy of trees and feeling a strong sense of privacy and mystery, even though the property was in a residential neighborhood near the center of town. The house was barely visible through the undergrowth, and we could not see the rear 200 ft. of the property. But we bought the place. The changing light among the trees convinced me that a garden here could be wonderful.

Making a garden, however, would be a challenge. In a climate balanced between temperate and tropical (Zone 8b, with winter lows of 20° F to 15° F), the south Louisiana native landscape is dominated by thick undergrowth and densely-spaced trees that grow over 100 ft. tall. Our almost-wild property was covered by a canopy of tall sweet gums and an impenetrable head-high thicket of elderberry, briars, and honeysuckle. No air stirred through the tangle of foliage, and the humidity bred swarms of mosquitoes. What's more, the growing conditions were far from ideal. The shade was deep, and under a thin layer of topsoil there was solid clay.

Planning the garden

We knew we would have to clear the undergrowth and many of the trees to make a garden, but we also wanted to retain the character that originally attracted us to the property—the feeling of mystery, change, surprise and refuge. The property reminded me of three painters—Monet, the Douanier Rousseau, and Jackson Pollock. Monet caught the play of light and shadow; we wanted the garden to catch it, too. As in Rousseau's paintings, where surprises emerge from the foliage, I wanted attractive plants to suddenly appear around a turn in a path. And, as in Pollock's paintings, we wanted layers to overlap everywhere, a series of curtains to create mystery.

We wanted the garden to have year-round interest yet reflect the native landscape, which is predominantly deciduous, with frequent accents of broadleaf evergreens, as well as flowers in subtle colors, mainly white and pastels. In other parts of the country, spring and summer bring waves of bloom, and the leaves blaze with color in the fall. Here, year-round interest takes effort. Native flowers are muted, and fall sometimes just doesn't happen—we seem to go from summer

In full bloom, the Florida flame azalea (*Rhododendron austrinum*) makes a subtle accent, more in keeping with naturalistic design than showier hybrid azaleas.

directly into winter with erratic changes in foliage color from year to year. Spring is the easiest season. In fact, there is such a wealth of fresh color and varied foliage all at once that it is easy to overdo and exaggerate. Summer is difficult. I planned to provide relief from the heavy, coarse greens of mature foliage by accenting the garden with plants whose foliage offers a diversity of color, shape and texture. For fall, I would include late-blooming plants. Although their flowers and colors are generally subtle, they make an impact when grouped in masses or set off by neighbors of contrasting color. Winter weather is inviting, with intense light and mild temperatures, but for variety and color I would have to plant evergreens, winter-flowering plants and fruiting shrubs. There is no peak time in the garden, and it changes daily, which makes its full character nearly impossible to record in photographs.

For two years, we hacked away the undergrowth and thinned the trees, eventually removing roughly half of the sweet gums (those with 8 in. trunk diameter or less) to accentuate the few natural openings in the canopy, and to create more play of light and shadow. Thinning transformed the property. We felt as if we were standing inside a gothic cathedral of soaring columns. Collectively, the sweet gums were magnificent.

We are landscape architects, trained to draw plans, and we teach at LSU where our students learn to draw plans, but this garden was designed by eye, far from pencil and paper. We laid a broad, winding path from the house to the back of the lot, following the few clearings among the trees, and reserved the rest of the land for planting. Jon has enjoyed giving me free rein with the choice of plants. To maintain the open character of the property, I intended to restrict myself to small trees, shrubs, and predominantly-low perennials. I took my time choosing and placing them, and I'm still adding plants today.

Trees and shrubs for shade

I planted several kinds of trees. Most were Japanese maples whose thin, fine foliage and open, sculptural branching serve as delicate screens throughout the garden. For variety and surprise, I added a few evergreen trees, such as Japanese evergreen oak *(Quercus glauca)* and deciduous trees with bold foliage such as the witch hazel (*Hamamelis virginiana*), with its undulating leaf edges, and pawpaw (*Asimina triloba*), with its curious purple flowers before the coarse-textured leaves appear in early spring.

Among the exotic trees I planted, two in particular stand out. One is the Japanese evergreen oak. It is a stunner. The branching resembles that of a large Japanese maple, the bark is light gray, and the foliage is a dense mass of lustrous, coarse leaves. I am amazed that it has not become more popular in the nursery trade. After 12 years, my specimens are 25 ft. high and wide. They are healthy and provide a dense, evergreen screen to the street. Another uncommon native beauty is the chalk maple (*Acer leucoderme*), a small deciduous tree whose leaves turn a soft but vibrant yellow every fall.

I planted a variety of shrubs at random throughout the garden. The deciduous species serve as seasonal accents, offering foliage, flowers, and in some cases, interesting fruits. The natives include beautyberry (*Callicarpa americana*), which has clusters of vivid lavender-purple fruits; sweetspire (*Itea virginica*), with long spikes of white, fragrant flowers; sweet shrub (*Calycanthus floridus*), whose rusty flowers produce a heady perfume that fills the air; honeysuckle azalea (*Rhododendron canescens*), which has tube-like white or pink flowers, and *R. austrinum,* whose yellow-orange flowers appear at the same time; and arrowwood *(Viburnum dentatum),* which bears white flowers in the spring. I also planted a number of exotic, deciduous shrubs, including winter honeysuckle (*Lonicera fragrantissima*), a highly

Gleaming raindrops weight down a flower stalk of a hybrid Louisiana iris which is used as an accent plant in the clearings.

A resurrection lily (*Kaempferia rotunda*) blooms amid groundcovers. The 2-in. flowers appear in spring, before the leaves.

fragrant species from China; wintersweet (*Chimonanthus praecox*), another Chinese native that flowers in winter before leaves appear; angel trumpet (*Brugmansia arborea*), a South American member of the nightshade family, which flowers in the hot, fall weather; and hybrid abutilons, small, tender, soft-woody shrubs that bloom in summer.

The evergreen shrubs are mainly broadleaf species. I've planted two camellias, *C. japonica* and *C. sasanqua*, natives of Japan that are available in hundreds of cultivars, most with showy pastel flowers; banana shrub (*Michelia figo*), a Chinese relative of the magnolia whose miniature, magnolia-like flowers have a strong banana fragrance; lusterleaf holly (*Ilex latifolia*), which has large, glossy, sharp-toothed leaves and red fruits; cherry laurel (*Prunus caroliniana*), a native with small, black fruits; and *Loropetalum chinense*, a Chinese member of the witch hazel family with showy, white, strap-like flowers in spring.

Photos: top, staff; bottom, Wayne Womack

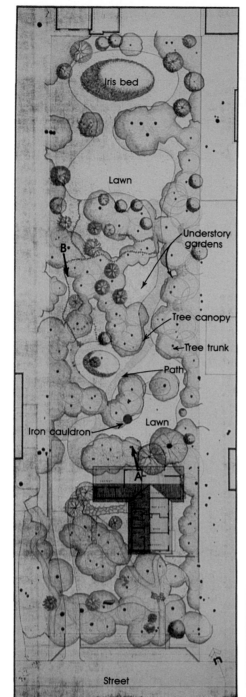

Site Plan

A footpath of stones crosses one of the rare clearings in the author's garden. The low perennials include ferns, gingers and irises. Two accent trees stand in the middle ground: a southern evergreen magnolia (*M. grandiflora*) with shiny evergreen leaves, and a honeysuckle azalea (*Rhododendron canescens*) in bloom. (Photo taken at B on site plan.)

A vigorous clump of an unknown crinum in bloom illustrates the impact that white flowers can make in deep shade.

The white, variegated leaves of a lacecap hydrangea (*Hydrangea microphylla* 'Tricolor') add variety to a corner of the garden dominated by foliage.

Low perennials for shade

Among the shrubs and trees I planted a nearly-solid carpet of low perennials. For foliage, the predominant plants are ferns—I grow 50 species. I love their feathery texture—it partially screens distant plants, making the garden look deeper, and it gives the garden a soft, lush base that seems semi-tropical. (For more about ferns, see "Favorite Ferns" on p. 62.) For accents I planted natives such as mayapple (*Podophyllum peltatum*), trillium (*Trillium* sp.), and Louisiana iris. Among the exotics in the garden, I particularly like members of the ginger family because the plants have lush, boldly textured foliage, fast growth and softly-colored fragrant flowers. I've been pleased with many plants from the ginger family, including *Alpinia, Costus, Curcuma, Globba, Hedychium,* and *Kaempferia.* All have proven hardy here, and remain largely unaffected by pests and diseases. Many genera from Asia and Europe are also at home here, including *Rohdea, Hosta* and

Aspidistra (the familiar indoor cast-iron plant). I've had special success with crinums, which form lily-like clumps of upright leaves and produce showy flowers. They rise dramatically from the ferns during the summer heat and are at their best in the fall when the heat is relentless. Those with white flowers seem to glow in the shade of the sweet gums.

I could make a new list of my favorite native plants every few days, as one group wanes and another comes into its glory, but I can mention a few that I would recommend to anyone with a suitable climate. Summersweet (*Clethra alnifolia*), a deciduous shrub, is a joy with its abundant white spires of bloom and rich fragrance (and is also hardy in Zone 5). The strawberry tree (*Euonymus americanus*), a small, barely-noticeable shrub much of the year, is spectacular in the fall with its almost shocking fruits of rose and orange. The starbush (*Illicium floridanum*) is a Louisiana native. I like its coarse, fragrant, evergreen foliage and the soft dusty red of

FAVORITE FERNS

Ferns are among my favorite plants—distinctive, like nothing else, and with a remarkable presence. Even the smallest ferns can project great energy in the crispness and strong arrangement of their foliage. Many species have fronds divided into pinnae (leaflike lobes), which may in turn be divided; and on the shady sites they generally favor, the play of light and shadow lends mystery to their wonderful feathery texture.

While I grow 50 species of ferns here in Baton Rouge, Louisiana, amid the roots and shade of tall trees, a few have proven to be exceptionally well-adapted. Among them are three natives, the marsh fern (*Thelypteris kunthii*), the royal fern (*Osmunda regalis*), and the lady fern (*Athyrium filix-femina*). The royal fern is hardy (Zone 3, -40°F) and majestic, with a dense fountain of green fronds that can stand 4 ft. to 5 ft. tall. The marsh fern spreads by creeping underground stems, with clusters of fronds at intervals, and it can be invasive, but it is easy to dig up clumps for transplanting. It stands up well to the intense heat of summer and fall. The lady fern, which is more delicate, has twice-divided fronds and is hardy in Zone 3.

Two of my stalwart ferns are exotics that have established themselves in the wild here. The Torres fern (*Thelypteris torresiana*), a lacy, light-green species, is from the Pacific Islands, but has naturalized across the southern U.S. The southern maidenhair fern (*Adiantum capillus-veneris*) has delicate, yellow-green lacy fronds with pinnae that are shaped like the leaves of the gingko tree (which is often called the maidenhair tree). There have been rare reports of plants growing wild in Louisiana.

A feather-like frond of the fern *Woodwardia orientalis* offers distinctive texture for the shade garden. Many fern species have fronds divided into leaf-like lobes called pinnae which can also be divided in turn (as shown here).

Two species of ferns growing side-by-side, the silvery Japanese painted fern (*Athyrium japonicum*) and the southern maidenhair fern (*Adiantum capillus-veneris*), suggest the wide range of fern foliage.

The rest of my mainstay ferns are imports. Two of them, the flakelet and vegetable ferns, verge on being invasive, but I handle the increase easily by giving plants to friends (and spreading the fern cult, I hope). The flakelet fern (*Hypolepsis repens*) is a large, vigorous species. The vegetable fern (*Diplazium esculentum*) has glossy leaves and spreads by stolons—shoots that run along the ground, take root, and send up fronds. Like the leaves of its namesake, the Japanese holly fern (*Cyrtomium falcatum*) makes a dense screen of shiny, tooth-edged foliage. Vigorous, with shiny fronds, the leatherleaf fern (*Rumohra adiantiformis*) is native on several continents in the southern hemisphere.

I have to mention two more ferns that fascinate me because they grow so slowly and carefully and seem to have such endurance. The species I have the greatest affection for is the Oriental chain fern (*Woodwardia orientalis*). I particularly enjoy the dramatic and lengthy unfolding of its copper-colored new fronds. It is a large, tough, leathery fern with an elegant disposition of fronds. While not a native, it has proven to be quite hardy here, though its usually-evergreen leaves are killed back by severe cold.

Another fern from the Orient, *Dryopteris sieboldii*, has proven much hardier than I had expected it to be. It is a very coarse-textured evergreen; the large leathery pinnae look like willow leaves. It is slow-growing, but becomes large and imposing with age.   —W.W.

SOURCES

The following mail-order nurseries offer extensive lists of ferns:

Fancy Fronds, 1911-4th Ave. West, Seattle, WA 98119. Catalog, $1.

Foliage Gardens, 2003-128th Ave. S.E., Bellevue, WA 98005. Catalog, $1.

Varga's Nursery, 2631 Pickertown Road, Warrington, PA 18976. List of species with brief descriptions, $1.

abundant star-like flowers in spring. There is a grove of starbush outside my bedroom, and on a cold morning I always look out to see if the leaves have curled—a sure sign that the temperature has dipped into the 20s. I grow two unusually-interesting native viburnums, *Viburnum nudum*, semi-evergreen, with an open-branching habit, and *V. acerifolium*, which is exceptionally vigorous and free-flowering. They wouldn't win a popularity contest against their showier cousins, but I find their reticence charming. I will admit to having one utter favorite native, the witch hazel (*Hamamelis virginiana*). Its toothed leaves and low, slender, spreading branches are lovely. I grow it close to the door of the house, so I can enjoy it regularly.

Maintenance

Though our property covers an acre, the garden is relatively undemanding to maintain. I don't like being a slave to weeding, pruning and spraying, and the naturalistic look of the garden spares me most of those burdens.

Happily, the main chores come up in winter, when the weather is best for outdoor work. Then I cut back all the herbaceous plants (spent ferns, gingers and the like), just before the first glimpse of early plants such as trilliums, mayapples, and snowdrops. I also spread a fresh layer of oak leaves, which tidies the garden, mulches the plants, and provides nutrition for the coming season. We collect several hundred bags of leaves around town each year, picking up those left at the curb for trash.

During the growing season, when the weather is often intolerably hot and humid, the garden demands very little care, aside from picking up an occasional fallen tree branch, or doing some judicious pruning to enhance the look of a plant. I allow the leaves to fall in the clearings and mow them along with the native grasses and herbs. In the borders the leaves sift in among the low plants and renew the mulch.

Contrasts enliven the author's shady garden: here the fronds of a lady fern (*Athyrium filix-femina*) touch the shiny leaves and red berries of *Ardisia crenata*, a low evergreen shrub that dies back in cold winters.

Enjoying the garden

One of the most telling reactions to the garden came from a friend who asked innocently, "When are you going to do something with the place?" It was a perfect compliment—I have sought an artless and natural look.

I garden for many reasons. Working in the soil and tending plants are among the most relaxing and satisfying activities I know, and since I visit the garden every day, the plants become intimate friends. The garden's constant change and evolution spare me from falling into routine responses to life. I am always amazed at people being depressed by fall or winter, when plants appear "dead." The transition from fall to winter is my favorite time in the garden, permeated by a wonderfully passive feeling as plants relax and let go for awhile to gear up for another boisterous spring.

I have always been drawn to shady gardens which emphasize light and texture and invite me to slow down and reflect. My garden is less a place to work than a place to sit and be thoughtful and enjoy. Instead of expecting a show of dramatic color, I've learned to enjoy looseness of structure and intermingling of forms. I've also come to enjoy sharing my haven with the wildlife it attracts. My property entertains raccoons, armadillos, opossums, king and garter snakes, box turtles, an army of lizards, towhees, woodpeckers, orioles, an occasional heron from a nearby swamp and once a family of wood ducks (they soon left, since I had no pond to hold them). This year brought the first visit of a prothonotary warbler family.

Above all I love the quiet moments when I can admire the garden and recognize its independence from me. True, I guide it a little—hopefully in its best interests—but my hand is small and the garden is vast. We are fellow travelers. ☐

Wayne Womack teaches landscape design at Louisiana State University and gardens in Baton Rouge, Louisiana.

Controlled Untidiness

Spillers and spires shape a cottage garden

by Alice Yarborough

My vision of an ideal cottage garden is one that appears to have been sown by Mother Nature. When my husband and I bought our property eight years ago, there were few signs that anyone had called the place home. On the eight acres of woods and pasture we found an old cellar hole, an aging lilac beside a tumbled chimney, and an old-fashioned poppy rose by a bit of sidewalk. I set out to create a colorful, meandering garden of perennial beds with gravel paths that were wide enough so my plants could spill over their edges.

Two public gardens influenced me. I especially love one, the cottage garden of Sissinghurst Castle in England. It's planted with what the guidebook calls "a controlled untidiness." I was also inspired by the University of Washington's Medicinal Herb Garden. In that quaint, lovely garden, I developed a taste for species plants that bear single, rather than double, flowers and display a loose, open habit of growth rather than the stiff, compact form common to many hybrids. Most of my choices are species plants or modern hybrids that have not undergone severe distortion of size, shape or bloom.

Achieving the perfect balance of paths and beds took some effort. I made the main paths 5 ft. wide and other paths only 3 ft. wide, but 3 ft. proved to be too narrow—the bushy, wet plants soaked our trouser legs as we walked by. My first beds were narrow enough for me to weed them from the paths, but my husband said the garden looked like a miniature golf course. So I eliminated some paths, consolidated beds and placed stepping stones in the larger beds for access.

Three broad groups of plants add color and form to my garden: tall accent plants; low, edge-breaking plants, and plants that attract desirable insects. The tall plants rise well overhead, lending drama to the garden. I don't feel obligated to put tall plants at the rear or middle of a bed. I frequently use a tall accent plant at the front of a bed. The low, edge-breaking plants in my garden help me achieve the controlled untidiness I'm looking for. They spill onto the paths, softening their edges and making the garden feel more intimate. The nectar plants attract butterflies, bumblebees and many other creatures whose bright colors and lively routines enrich the garden. All three kinds of plants can add grace to your garden, whatever its style. I'll tell you about a few of my favorites.

Lofty plants

The tall plants, at 6 ft. to 12 ft., are dramatic, so I use them sparingly, but in one bed I did group three that bloom in sequence: 6-ft. tall foxgloves (*Digitalis*), which bloom in late May and early June, followed by 8-ft. tall, golden-flowered inula (*Inula magnifica*), which blooms in late June and early July and 8-ft. tall, red-flowered hollyhocks (*Alcea rosea*), which carry on from July into September.

One of the imposing plants in my garden prefers shade. Goatsbeard (*Aruncus dioicus*) grows 6 ft. tall and has gracefully arching stalks of tiny, creamy white flowers in June and July. Because the elegant, compound leaves of this shade-lover are attractive throughout the growing season, I planted it alongside a shady path.

Joe-Pye weed (*Eupatorium purpureum*) is the most exciting plant in my garden. Growing 8 ft. tall and about half as wide, my two clumps are strikingly beautiful long before they bloom. An established plant sends up thirty to forty erect, red-tinged stalks that carry whorls of green, lance-shaped leaves. In late July Joe-Pye weed turns into a fluffy-headed dazzler—butterflies and bees mob its 10-in. clusters of dusty rose flowers. The blooms last from four to five weeks.

White loosestrife (*Lysimachia ephemerum*) is a well-behaved member of a notoriously invasive genus. Its numerous airy spires of small white flowers rise to a height of 5 ft. or 6 ft. The bloom period, which starts in July, goes on for weeks and weeks, as the flower stalks continue lengthening. White loosestrife likes sun and plenty of moisture. Grayish, narrow leaves

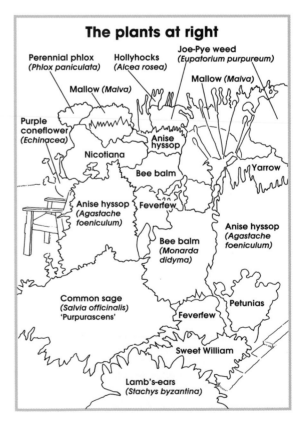

The plants at right

Perennial phlox
(*Phlox paniculata*)

Hollyhocks
(*Alcea rosea*)

Joe-Pye weed
(*Eupatorium purpureum*)

Mallow (*Malva*)

Mallow (*Malva*)

Purple coneflower
(*Echinacea*)

Anise hyssop

Nicotiana

Bee balm

Yarrow

Anise hyssop
(*Agastache foeniculum*)

Feverfew

Anise hyssop
(*Agastache foeniculum*)

Bee balm
(*Monarda didyma*)

Common sage
(*Salvia officinalis*
'Purpurascens')

Petunias

Feverfew

Sweet William

Lamb's-ears
(*Stachys byzantina*)

Edging plants spill onto paths wide enough to accommodate a chair. (For the names of the plants shown here, see the drawing at left.) The author laid out her garden in paths and beds and shaped it with tall and short plants.

All photos: David McDonald

Ground covers creep across stepping-stones of sliced logs. The view rises from ground-hugging variegated and purple sages to yellow-flowered coreopsis, through red hollyhocks and bee balm to the woods beyond the woodshed.

Lilac-colored asters soften the edges of a gravel path and envelop a potted lavender.

add considerably to the plant's quiet charm. Because of its understated colors, white loosestrife shows to best advantage in stands of two to four plants spaced about 2½ ft. apart.

Patience is necessary when growing white loosestrife. My plants looked so wispy their first two years that I nearly trashed them. But by their third summer, I had large, flower-laden clumps of great beauty.

Pink mallow (*Malva alcea* var. *fastigiata*), a particular favorite of mine, is an overly efficient self-sower. Bushy, loosely branching, 6-ft. plants carry an abundance of clear pink, single flowers for about six weeks in midsummer.

Mulleins, also called verbascums, pop up all over the garden. I grow half a dozen members of this large genus, and I wish I had more. Two I especially enjoy are biennials, blooming their second summer from June-sown seed. Moth mullein (*Verbascum blattaria* 'Alba') sends up delicate 6-ft. to 8-ft. spires of white blossoms over a flat clump of dark green leaves. Although less graceful, *V. bombyciferum* 'Arctic Summer' is endearingly quaint. Its silvery basal leaves are big and floppy, and its supremely fleecy 5-ft. to 6-ft. stalks are studded with yellow flowers. *V. olympicum* and its hybrid forms make imposing 8-ft. to 12-ft. spires of yellow blossoms above 3-ft. wide rosettes of grayish leaves.

Anise hyssop (*Agastache foeniculum*) is easy to grow. From midsummer into fall, its shrubby, 5-ft. stalks of dark green leaves support numerous 3-in. to 5-in. spikes of tiny lavender flowers. It blooms the first year from seed, and a big, blossoming clump of it, full of honeybees and butterflies, is a fine sight. Its leaves smell and taste like anise.

Edge-breakers

Spreading, low-growing plants such as pinks, lady's-mantle, and sweet alyssum are plants more than willing to help gardeners win the war against severe and tidy edges. Their flowers flow onto path and patio, calling to mind the nasturtiums that spread onto the paths in the garden of Claude Monet, the Impressionist painter.

One of my favorite edge-breakers is lady's-mantle (*Alchemilla mollis*), which grows 12 in. high and bears chartreuse flowers above its downy, scalloped leaves. Lady's-mantle needs midsummer shearing to keep it from becoming a relentless self-sower. I also like the pale yellow *Coreopsis* 'Moonbeam' and the soft pink hardy geranium 'Mavis Simpson'. Neither of these obliging summer-long bloomers flop over or self-sow. I find the nasturtium 'Whirlybirds', which is less rampant than those in Monet's garden, a good choice for planting alongside my paths.

Another fine edger, the little Mexican daisy (Erigeron karvinskianus), is a lacy-leaved, foot-high plant that bears small pink and white daisies throughout summer. It likes sun and is drought-resistant.

I like the go-with-everything colors of the low-growing common sage (Salvia officinalis)—both the purple-leaved and the green-and-cream variegated forms. These sun-lovers need no fertilizer and almost no water. In my garden they hold their leaves year-round. I keep some live buds on each branch when I prune in April, because sage is reluctant to break new buds from old wood. My oldest plants have a 5-ft. spread, although they're only 20 in. high.

Golden marjoram (Origanum vulgare 'Aureum') is an herb I grow in close company with the sages. The sages' muted colors set off the marjoram's glowing chartreuse foliage. If I prune it hard in early spring, by May it's a 1-ft. high mound of tiny leaves, gradually spreading without becoming invasive. For best leaf color I plant it in full sun.

Plants for desirable insects

Mine is an insect lover's garden where any plant that attracts bees, moths or butterflies gets bonus points. On warm days in early September, when bumblebees jostle Red Admiral butterflies for space on the sunflowers, and katydids stalk the late-blooming phlox, I enjoy my finest moments in the garden.

Every spring I sow seeds of the 4-ft. tall rose-, white- and pink-flowering annual nicotiana 'Sensation'. On summer evenings its tubular flowers pro-duce a strong, spicy-sweet perfume, an invitation to nectar-loving moths.

I value sedums, yarrows, monardas and centranthus for their appeal to bees and butterflies. The blue-flowering borage, which self-sows, is a food plant for Painted Lady butterfly caterpillars. Old-fashioned candytuft self-sows freely, doing double duty as a butterfly plant and a charming path edger. □

Alice Yarborough gardens in Carnation, Washington.

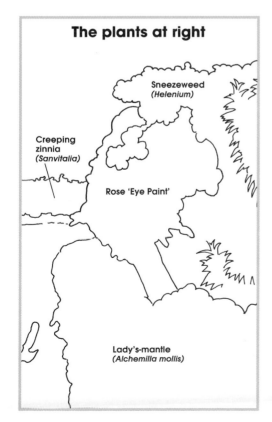

The plants at right

Sneezeweed (Helenium)

Creeping zinnia (Sanvitalia)

Rose 'Eye Paint'

Lady's-mantle (Alchemilla mollis)

Low plants soften the edges of a gravel path, while tall plants make a dramatic background. (For the names of the plants, see the drawing at left.)

A No-Lawn Curbscape

Year-round beauty with minimal upkeep

by Tom Mannion

Streetside landscapes in residential areas are often nothing more than unused lawns. Distinguished only by a few flowers ringing a mailbox pole, they blend anonymously with the neighborhood greensward. I think masses of striking plants that offer a new palette of flower and foliage color each season are much more interesting than grass. And, they can require no more maintenance than a lawn.

A look at a job my colleague, Louise Kane, and I did in suburban Maryland a few years back can give you an idea of what's involved. As the photos and drawing show, this was a big property, but we've found that our approach also works well for smaller streetside areas.

A massive expanse of sparsely growing grass bordered the 350 ft. of street in front of Lee and René Ewing's house. From the street, the rocky terrain sloped slightly up to the house; an 11-ft.-wide driveway divided the area into two unequal sections. Small clusters of hickory, dogwood, oak and black gum trees stood out in the barren landscape, awkward survivors of the developer's overzealous bulldozer. We could have resurrected the lawn, but the Ewings didn't want to invest in an irrigation system and the ongoing care a lawn would require. They regarded the lawn as an uninteresting nuisance, dutifully maintaining it, but never walking on it except at the back end of a lawn mower.

Their request was simple: They wanted to be greeted by a more imaginative landscape and to do less work. At our initial meeting, we suggested eliminating the lawn and replacing it with lower-maintenance, drought-tolerant plants that would be seasonally colorful and interesting year round. The Ewings wholeheartedly agreed with our approach.

Design

As Louise and I analyzed the site, the design parameters became clear. Along the

July—Before this meadow-like landscape was planted, this front yard was just a worn-out lawn and a few patches of trees. Now large masses of drought-tolerant herbaceous perennials sweep along the road, presenting car-stopping displays throughout the year. Here, black-eyed Susans and red hibiscus cover the ground in July, just two years after planting. (Taken at A on site plan.)

length of the street, the lawn had no distinct beginning or end, and the clusters of trees, 25 ft. from the street, cut the area off from the rest of the property. The streetside plantings would be barely visible from the house, which is set back 65 ft. from the road. So they had to be sizable enough in scale to be enjoyed through the windows of cars passing by at 30 mph. Small groups of plants or too much variety would slip by unnoticed. Larger-scale plantings also would create a continuous vista from one end of the property to the other, encouraging onlookers to see the garden as a unit.

The new plantings would be far from existing hose bibbs. Without an irrigation system, they'd have to survive with our 45 in. of average annual rainfall, and to withstand Maryland's annual droughts, which sometimes come in midsummer but always in September. The Ewings were willing to irrigate by hand for a season until the plants got established, but felt that

more than that would be a nasty chore.

Our idea was to create the feeling of a large meadow emerging from the edge of a woods and flowing down to the street. Natural meadows look like they've been left to their own devices rather than groomed and pruned by human hands. Unmowed grasses predominate, dotted with many different broadleaf plants. To us, this informality is relaxing and visually pleasing.

We didn't want to replicate a natural meadow, though. From the street, too much variety would make the garden look disjointed and wouldn't produce the eye-catching blocks of seasonal colors and textures we wanted. So with natural meadows as our inspiration, we envisioned a more stylized, simpler planting adjacent to the street. We'd include just a few different kinds of herbaceous perennials, planted in large, drifting masses of one species apiece. Each mass would have a distinctive leaf or flower texture and color, but we hoped that the curved

October — Layers of contrasting color and texture rise from the curb to the woods. The silvery-gray lamb's-ears are backed up by tan fountain-grass plumes and red-leaved euonymus. Newly planted golden-rain and dogwood trees create a gradual transition between the new plantings and the woodland. (Taken at B on site plan.)

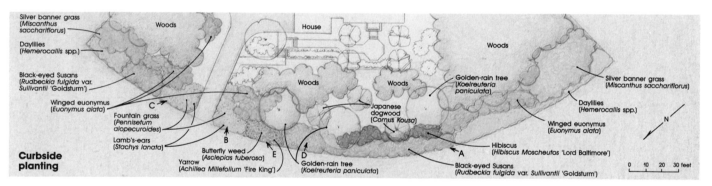

Curbside planting

Silver banner grass (*Miscanthus sacchariflorus*)
Daylilies (*Hemerocallis spp.*)
Black-eyed Susans (*Rudbeckia fulgida* var. *Sullivantii* 'Goldsturm')
Winged euonymus (*Euonymus alata*)
Fountain grass (*Pennisetum alopecuroides*)
Lamb's-ears (*Stachys lanata*)
Butterfly weed (*Asclepias tuberosa*)
Yarrow (*Achillea Millefolium* 'Fire King')
Golden-rain tree (*Koelreuteria paniculata*)
Woods
House
Japanese dogwood (*Cornus Kousa*)
Golden-rain tree (*Koelreuteria paniculata*)
Silver banner grass (*Miscanthus sacchariflorus*)
Daylilies (*Hemerocallis spp.*)
Winged euonymus (*Euonymus alata*)
Hibiscus (*Hibiscus Moscheutos* 'Lord Baltimore')
Black-eyed Susans (*Rudbeckia fulgida* var. *Sullivantii* 'Goldsturm')

0 10 20 30 feet

edges would make the plantings flow together. To integrate the existing trees into the new landscape, we planned to mass deciduous shrubs between the trees and the meadow, and intersperse a few new trees in the meadow.

Plant selection

The northwest-facing yard, partly shaded in the morning and in bright sunshine all afternoon, is amenable to a wide variety of plants. So we chose plants with attention-grabbing flower colors or textures, varieties that would need no summer irrigation (except to establish them), infrequent weeding and little fertilizing. To reduce weeding, we used mostly tall plants rather than ground-hugging ones — weeds growing under taller plants are less noticeable.

Our idea of seasonal color is a bit different from the popular notion of constant bloom throughout the garden, with different plants flowering each season. We, too, try to have something striking happening

during each season, but we pace the garden, with slow times between the knock-your-socks-off events. These respites create a feeling of great anticipation, like an unopened present. And to us, the texture and color of dried foliage and flower heads and bare branches in the winter are as interesting as splashy summer blooms are.

We filled in the thinner stand of woods in front of the house with three golden-rain trees (*Koelreuteria paniculata*), which will grow almost as tall as the existing trees, and three Japanese dogwoods (*Cornus Kousa*), which form a lower story. The golden-rain's pendulous golden flower clusters bloom in June; the dogwoods display their creamy-white flowers in June and July, yellow and scarlet leaves in the fall, and bright-red fruits in the winter.

We planted winged euonymus, or burning bush (*Euonymus alata*), in front of the wooded areas. This deciduous shrub slowly grows 7 ft. to 8 ft. tall and 10 ft. to 15 ft. wide. Attractive year round, it's especially

spectacular in the fall, covered with bright-red leaves. Its twiggy, asymmetrical horizontal branches look splendid in the winter, too. It's also very drought-tolerant.

Three plant combinations form the backbone of the herbaceous portion of the meadow. Southwest of the driveway, we planted a small mass of hibiscus (*Hibiscus Moscheutos* 'Lord Baltimore') behind a larger, central mass of black-eyed Susans (*Rudbeckia fulgida* var. Sullivantii 'Goldsturm'). The plate-size, fire-engine-red flowers of the hibiscus successfully compete for attention with the overly bright, harsh-gold blooms of the black-eyed Susans. And the neatly mounding leaves and flowers of the black-eyed Susans camouflage the gangly hibiscus stalks. This raucous red-and-gold composition is intense throughout July and August, just the right months of the year for hot colors. Even after the ray flowers fall off, a sea of attractive black eyes persists through the winter. We also planted black-eyed Su-

March—'King Alfred' daffodils bloom among cut-back fountain grass, a welcome relief from the stark winter landscape. (Photos above and below taken at C on site plan.)

The new herbaceous perennials and trees, spaced far enough apart to accommodate their size at maturity, were barely visible just after planting. Three years later, they had filled in completely. (Taken at D on site plan.)

August—Tan plumes of fountain grass, planted on either side of the driveway, droop over a silvery-gray ground cover of lamb's-ears.

sans alone on the other side of the drive.

Flanking both sides of the driveway, a small planting of lamb's-ears (*Stachys lanata*) borders a large mass of fountain grass (*Pennisetum alopecuroides*). The fountain grass, which grows about 2½ ft. tall, defines the driveway entrance without obstructing the view from one end of the meadow to the other. Its feathery plumes bloom from July to November. The luminescent, pale-gray leaves of the lamb's-ears carpet the ground and make the edges of the drive easy to see at night. Its lavender flowers bloom in June and July, and its fuzzy-textured leaves sharply contrast with those of the fountain grass.

The third plant combination, orange-flowered butterfly weed (*Asclepias tuberosa*) with pale-red flowered yarrow (*Achillea Millefolium* 'Fire King'), is smaller in scale. This color combination sounds dreadful and I wasn't sure how it would look, but it's turned out quite lovely (photo, facing page). It reminds me of a bowl of red

grapes and oranges. Both bloom in June.

At the front edge of the meadow, large masses of dwarf, peach-flowered daylilies (*Hemerocallis* spp.) bloom in June and July, their swordlike foliage contrasting with the medium-coarse leaves of the adjacent black-eyed Susans. The daylilies die back in early fall, but are underplanted with 2,000 daffodils (*Narcissus* 'Ice Follies'), whose pale-yellow and white flowers brighten the area in early spring.

We also packed 1,000 'King Alfred' daffodils among the fountain grass, and scattered hundreds of *Allium aflatunense* 'Purple Splendor' and Spanish bluebells (*Scilla hispanica*) through the hibiscus. This show of life in March is reassuring, particularly around a late sleeper like hibiscus, which doesn't show its head until June.

Silver banner grass (*Miscanthus sacchariflorus*) frames the whole picture, greeting visitors at both ends of the property. Its slender leaves contrast with the predominately broadleafed plants in the rest of

the meadow, and accent the start and finish of this planting, clearly defining it as a unit. Like euonymus, it's an intermediate height. Its silvery-white plumes highlight the garden in October and November, when its green foliage becomes light tan.

Planting

Our company's crew, under the direction of John Cimabue, planted the curbscape in August, which gave the plants enough time to put out new roots before winter. To prepare the area for planting, we killed the lawn with the herbicide Roundup and we tilled in the remnants twice. We salvaged some native rocky clay soil from an excavation in the Ewings' backyard, first checking that it could be tilled into a workable soil. We spread a 6-in. to 8-in. layer of this soil, tilled it in, combed it with a metal rake pulled behind a tractor to remove large stones, and retilled it.

Next we planted the trees and the euonymus. We mulched around them with 2 in. of shredded hardwood bark and between them with 3 in. of bark. We planted the perennials and grasses through the mulch, piling no more than 2 in. of it around their crowns. This clay soil is fertile, so we didn't fertilize at planting time, although on other sites we sometimes use a slow-release fertilizer. In October, we planted the bulbs, a fairly easy job amidst the widely spaced plants.

We spaced the plants so that they would fill in the entire area when they reached their anticipated mature size. Overplanting would just result in the near-impossible task of thinning later on. The ivy that we planted on the slope

June—A small patch of orange-flowered butterfly weed and pale-red flowered yarrow creates a striking splash of color. (Taken at E on site plan.)

above the meadow area was one exception—it eventually grows in a tangle anyway, so we planted it 8 in. apart to encourage a quick cover. But we bought medium or large plants of everything else, so they'd fill in fast: 1-qt. yarrow, lamb's-ears and black-eyed Susans; 8-ft.- to 15-ft.-tall trees; 2½-ft.-tall euonymus; 1-gal. grasses and hibiscus; and bare-root daylilies and butterfly weed. Smaller or bare-root plants would have cost less, but would have taken an extra year to fill in.

Even with bigger plants, the newly planted landscape looked ludicrous—just a huge sweep of mulch speckled with tiny bits of grass. The banner-grass plants were 6 ft. apart, the fountain grass 4 ft., and the black-eyed Susans and daylilies 3 ft. Fortunately, the Ewings were prepared for this near-empty look and were satisfied to anticipate the results. The plants started to mesh two years after planting. By the third year, all but the euonymus had grown into a solid mass.

Maintenance

For a landscape like this, maintenance is most time-consuming during the two years after planting, requiring diligent weeding and watering. In the summers, the Ewings hand-weeded one or two times per month, just tossing the weeds on the mulch. They also sprinkler-irrigated the plants once a week, soaking them until the soil was wet 1 in. to 2 in. deep, which is ample water in this soil. Now they irrigate only during droughts. Even during the 1988 dry spell, only the black-eyed Susans required irrigation for survival.

Starting the first winter, and each winter thereafter, the grasses and perennials in a planting like this need to be mowed to remove their dried tops, making room for new, springtime growth. "Mowing" the meadow actually makes it sound too easy. In fact, it's a hard chore. Low maintenance in this landscape doesn't mean no work. The Ewings cut down the grass foliage with a chain saw, and the black-eyed Susans and other herbaceous plants with power shears. Power tools like these aren't necessary, but they do make it much easier to barrel through a large planting. To avoid tiptoeing through newly emerging daffodils, the Ewings mow in February. Without daffodils, they could wait until March. As the plants have matured, hauling out the huge quantity of prunings has become quite a chore. Now a landscape-maintenance company does the winter cleanup.

Recently the Ewings have decided to cut down the banner grass in November instead of February, sacrificing several months of winter beauty. By late winter, bits of its dried foliage have traveled up and down the street, littering neighboring lawns. Unlike with the more anonymous woodland leaves, everyone knows whose landscape loosed the banner grass.

Even with the annual mowing, ongoing maintenance is far less work for the Ewings than their previous lawn-care ritual was. The closely knit plants suppress most weeds; occasionally Lee and René pull out a few dandelions. More often, they have to remove volunteer plants that have seeded in the wrong part of the landscape: lamb's-ears in the yarrow, black-eyed Susans in the daylilies. Dis-

ease and insect pests have been almost nonexistent. The Ewings feed the daffodils after bloom; the rest of the plants look healthy so far with no fertilizing, but they'll feed them if they show symptoms of nutrient deficiency. They cut off the ratty-looking flowers of the lamb's-ears in early summer, making a surprisingly beautiful arrangement of them. About the time the euonymus's red leaves take center stage, they cut back the hibiscus, which detracts from the view.

Once the plants grow together in a landscape like this, it's almost impossible to remulch. But even when the plants were younger, we avoided fresh mulch. It makes a landscape look too new. When the initial mulch breaks down, the Ewings may choose to mulch again. In the future, they may have to divide or replace older plants. Then the volunteer plants will be an ample resource.

The Ewings' curbscape has become a wildlife haven over the years. Goldfinches, cardinals and a pair of bluebirds frequent the garden year round. The air above the meadow dances all summer with butterflies and bees. Rabbits, deer and a fox have been spotted, heading into the woods. No longer do the Ewings spend their weekends enslaved to an unattractive lawn. They enjoy the seasonal changes in their landscape. And long after the daffodils have bloomed or the euonymus leaves have fallen off, they still remember them with pleasure. □

Tom Mannion is a landscape designer and owner of Tom Mannion Associates in Arlington, Virginia.

One-Woman Show

Breathtaking display on a suburban lot

by Alice Menard

Editors' note: When free-lance photographer Chuck Crandall sent us photographs of Alice Menard's garden in Lakeside, California, we first remarked at the abundance of bloom. Massed in beds around the lawn and mounded in containers near the house are thousands of plants covered with flowers that gleam in the sun and beckon from the shade. This garden is a flower lover's delight, saturating the senses with color and fragrance from early spring through late fall. We also admired the impeccable grooming: every plant is upright, staked and pruned, with dead flowers removed, and the lawn is precisely trimmed and edged.

We contacted Alice and learned that she had single-handedly created this stunning display on an ordinary suburban lot. So we asked her to write about it, explaining what she had done and sharing what she had learned. But before she could complete the article, she was killed in a freak accident. In recent years, Alice had depended on the garden to earn her living, in part by opening it to the public and giving tours. We decided to present this photographic tour of Alice's garden; her daughter, Marilyn Lougy, helped us adapt Alice's handwritten notes to accompany the pictures on the following pages.

Photos: above, Alice Menard; all others, © Chuck Crandall

When we moved to this suburb of San Diego 40 years ago, there were fewer than a dozen homes along a mile-long stretch of dirt road. Our 100-ft. by 150-ft. lot had no landscaping, just a lawn and a few trees. I'd grown up in California, but my parents were both English, and some of my earliest memories are of my mother's beautiful English-style flower garden. Like hers, my garden combines perennials, annuals, shrubs, vines and thousands of bulbs. I have hundreds of kinds of plants, and try to have something in bloom throughout the year (see photo on facing page).

Perennials are the backbone of the garden. Some of my favorites are agapanthus (the large clump of purple flowers at center above), coreopsis, yarrow, iberis, alyssum 'Basket of Gold', columbines, irises, phlox and daylilies. Among the perennials, I've planted narcissus and daffodils, spring starflowers, wood hyacinths, snowflakes, and other bulbs. As soon as their flower stalks die back, I'm quick to plant annuals in between the yellowing leaves. Some of my favorite annuals are white alyssum (edging the front of the bed) and purple lobelia (bottom corner). Other favorites are marigolds, red salvias and orange cosmos, because I like the sunny colors—yellow, red and orange. Many South African bulbs—sparaxis, babianas, tritonias, freesias, ixias, montbretias—add to the summer show of color.

Studying the patterns in nature helps me decide how to arrange the plants. For example, wild plants never grow in rows or circles or straight lines, but in patches that blend together, making tapestries of colors and textures. I try to create this effect in the garden. Also, I mix plants of different heights and let them flow together, rather than making stairsteps with tall plants in back and short ones in front.

More than 200 kinds of roses play a part in my garden (left). Climbing roses cover the fences, and Miniatures and Floribundas mingle with perennials in my borders and beds. Most "rose gardens" look stiff and unattractive to me, since people often plant roses in rows with no thought for the color combinations. In creating my own rose garden, I planted several plants of each variety, to make masses of color. I put the Floribunda bushes in the foreground, because they have a graceful shape that takes your eye from the less attractive Hybrid Teas. Here in southern California, roses bloom for a nine-month season, starting in late March. Some are still flowering when I prune the bushes in early January.

I mulch the rose garden with bark chips to give it a well-groomed look. The mulch also helps keep the roots cooler in summer and holds moisture. In the rest of the garden, I spread leaves, lawn clippings, horse manure and other organic matter onto the beds, tucking the heavier chunks under shrubs. You never see a humus pile in nature, and you won't see one in my garden either. Composting in place is an easy way to improve the soil's consistency and to add nutrients.

In my shady area, the lath strips run north and south so the sunlit areas keep shifting all day. Here I grow lush maidenhair and leather-leaf ferns and durable aspidistras for foliage; camellias and azaleas; and primroses, impatiens and begonias for masses of color. In summer, lush hanging baskets filled with begonias, impatiens and lobelia fill the air with color (shown in bloom at right). I use these plants in pots on the ground also, to brighten the dark green foliage with cheerful bloom.

I grow many plants in containers, such as a rose-colored phlox, yellow pansies and marigolds, purple ageratums, white alyssum, and pink petunias (left). That way I can move them around when they come into bloom. It's wonderful to set them near the front door. I also use potted plants to fill spaces in the garden where the roots from nearby trees or shrubs prevent planting in the ground. I mix soil for the containers by combining good garden soil, peat moss, redwood bark and horse manure. Mixing soil is like making a kettle of soup. A good cook never measures. You learn to have a feel for what's right.

Visitors often ask how many gardeners I have, but I have no help. I do all the maintenance myself, such as deadheading the coreopsis (right). My motto is "A stitch in time saves nine": I'm happiest if I keep on top of the work, and I never let things get out of hand. □

A Small Pleasure Garden

Ornamentals brighten every inch of a city lot

by Walter Bull

What I like best in gardening is richness. In spite of a difficult site, I've filled my townhouse property to overflowing with plants—out front in two small plots that flank the entrance, along the sides where sun is scarce and the property lines are 5 ft. away, and out back on a terraced slope that looks down on the house. When I ran out of ground, I converted the swimming pool into a lily pond and started growing ornamentals in containers that I tucked into unused niches and moved around the garden as the seasons changed. Here and there, I installed sculptures and whimsies. The garden provides year-round color, constant change and a great diversity of shapes and textures. It also gives me an opportunity for self-expression and creativity. I'm still adding plants, and I expect to continue. The garden will never be finished.

In the beginning

Here in Columbia, South Carolina (on the boundary between USDA Zones 7 and 8), we can garden 360 days out of the year—the other five days we stay inside because of the heat. Our winters are very mild. In fact, we wouldn't know a frost heave if we saw it. We can have color in every season, with some effort. Summer is the most difficult time, but we have plants that tolerate the heat and offer color, provided we water and mulch with care. Our long season has drawbacks, though. Roses bloom right into January, but they also suffer year-round from the fungal disease blackspot.

When my wife and I moved into our new house in 1982, the only living things were one clump of irises, six wax myrtles and fire ants. If there had ever been topsoil, it was long gone. We had a swimming pool and lots of red clay on a 60-ft. wide lot with neighbors close by on both sides. We enjoyed our new neighborhood, an urban renewal project of townhouses near the capitol and the University of South Carolina, but we needed a garden.

Color brightens the garden in every season. At left, the purple spires of Mexican bush salvia (Salvia leucantha) crowd the yellow blooms of a swamp sunflower (Helianthus angustifolia) in late summer.

Just ornamentals out front

I made a false start in the front yard. The staircase to the front door is flanked by 15-ft. square plots inside a low brick wall. We filled both plots with daylilies, which are Southern favorites—they're easy to grow and almost impossible to kill. But when the plants died back in mid-winter, the front yard was nothing but pine straw mulch. I liked the daylilies, but after two or three years, I decided I wanted to have color in the front garden year-round.

I replanted the front yard with bulbs, perennials, roses and conifers. Espaliered up the sides of the steps and serving as the backdrop for the entire cottage garden is pyracantha, a thorny shrub with white flowers in spring and showy red berries all winter. In each plot, three cypresses and a butterfly bush (Buddleia davidii) provide structure and green all year long.

Seen from the third story of the house, the author's backyard garden is rich in colors, shapes and textures. A winding path climbs the terraced slope. The pond is an artfully transformed swimming pool: lilies and sedges grow in containers set atop submerged platforms, while flagstones and potted plants surround the water.

In the wintertime, tulips, daffodils, pansies and hyacinths bloom among the bright green Nippon daisies and ornamental kales and cabbages. Daylilies, Siberian irises and lilies flower in the summer.

Plants in narrow passages

Necessity prompted me to make a container allée along the left side of the house. There was no soil, just a 3-ft. brick wall and a walkway. I find that almost any plant, even a shrub or a tree, can grow in a container. (Of course, winters are mild here, so the roots are safe from cold injury.) I have magnolias, azaleas and camellias in containers along the walkway, their branches espaliered against the wall of the house. I have roses, conifers, viburnums, holly grapes (*Mahonia* spp.), vitexes, sedums, bulbs and annuals growing in containers atop the brick wall. The container garden has color all year. In the late winter and early spring, the camellias and azaleas bloom. One of the most beautiful plants to flower in January and February is the daphne, a graceful shrub which grows better for me in a container than in the soil. The mahonias bloom throughout the summer, while the roses start flowering in late April and go at least until December. In the spring, tulips, daffodils, iris and crocuses are wonderful.

One of my greatest gardening pleasures is watering containers in the summertime. I've lit the entire yard so I can garden at night. The lights for the container garden are on the side of the house, and produce unique shadows that make watering a double treat.

Along the right hand side of the house, I've made a shade garden. The sun is blocked by our house, the neighbor's house, and a rose-covered arbor. A chest-high wall on our side stands 12 in. away from a higher wall on our neighbor's side. In the 12-in. wide plot between the walls, I grow plants that are usually found in woodland gardens. It's an exquisite place for tiny things like trilliums. They meet us eye to eye. The plot includes Jack-in-the-pulpit, pansies, white-flowered lamium, miniature jonquils, blue-eyed grass and a little bronze hippo. In a narrow strip of soil along the house, I grow daffodils, jonquils, grasses and canna lilies. It is interesting to grow cannas in the shade. I am told it can't be done, but my plants haven't heard that, and

the beautiful red flowers and broad, green leaves are gorgeous against the grey wall of the house.

Around and in the pool

The container garden and the shade garden lead to the pool and terraces in the backyard. If you walk through the shade garden, your first view of the backyard is a bronze, life-size figure of a boy playing a flute. He's sitting on the edge of a terrace with his feet dangling. On the other side of the house, the container garden leads to a wrought iron gate almost covered with Carolina jessamine. Through the gate you see a small

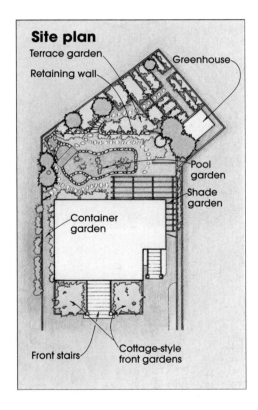

Site plan
Terrace garden
Retaining wall
Greenhouse
Pool garden
Shade garden
Container garden
Front stairs
Cottage-style front gardens

waterfall and a canopy of wax myrtles sheltering a bronze Buddha. The Buddha holds an alms basin, which I fill with water for the birds.

The swimming pool was designed to invite bathers to just float there with a wine glass, but gardening has taken it over. I got interested in water lilies and bought a barrel to grow them in. Soon I had four barrels. I bought a bathtub for more water lilies. Then I dug a little pond and waterproofed it with a plastic liner. I liked the water lilies so much that I tried lotuses. Then I tried fish. When I ran out of room, I decided I liked plants and fish more than I liked floating with a wine glass, so I turned the swimming pool into a pond.

The pool was too deep for water plants, so I put them in containers on platforms made of cement blocks and plastic trash cans turned upside down. I can redo the pond garden anytime I like by getting in the water and moving the pots. I also get into the pool to deadhead and fertilize the plants. The fish are very affectionate: they come up and nibble on me when I'm in the water.

Around the pool I grow a garden of perennials, bulbs, shrubs and small trees. The garden is divided into sections by flower color, from deep red to light pink. Throughout, I grow morning-glories, agapanthus, plumbago and other plants with blue flowers, to unify the colors. I got the idea for the agapanthus from a painting by Monet.

Many of the pool-garden plants grow in pots. They include viburnums, tea olives, magnolias, cypress trees, Japanese magnolias and roses. I'm also trying peonies, which historically have not been a southern plant because our soil stays too warm for the cold dormant period they need. In pots, the roots receive enough cold. There's even a potted sequoia.

I love potted plants. I can move them to fill a bare spot or add color as the garden changes with the seasons. I can rearrange the garden every day, and the plants never suffer transplanting shock. I can bring tender plants into the house in the winter and continue to enjoy them. Bringing plants inside makes the house an extension of the garden. I think interior decorating and gardening have a lot in common, and I like to strengthen the connection by using garden colors and floral motifs in the house.

Another advantage of container growing is that invasive plants can be kept in check. Wisteria, which is a rampant grower here in the South, grows nicely in a container and stays put. I'm training a potted wisteria in an arch over the pool. Ivy also does well in containers.

The terrace garden

I've terraced the slope behind the pool with a 3-ft. high wall. Chrysanthemums cascade from the terrace, and taller plants such as helianthus rise high above the wall. Visitors look up to the terrace garden and are drawn to explore it. At one end of the wall, steps ascend to a path that winds across the terrace. I made the path circuitous

Illustration: **Heather Brine Lambert**

A cottage-garden wealth of plants fills a small plot in the front yard beside the entrance stairs. Their branches spread and tied, pyracanthas cover the railing and the lattice. Cypress trees provide a backdrop for the purple flowers of a butterfly bush and a clump of cascading white daisies.

because I want visitors to slow down, see the garden from many vantage points, and find surprises at every turn. Sculptures hide here and there, among them an oversized bronze frog that makes me feel Lilliputian.

The pond and terrace gardens form a sanctuary, enclosed by walls and plants. The walls are almost covered with espaliers of magnolias, camellias, azaleas, and 'Mermaid' and 'Lady Banks' roses. Butterflies and hummingbirds visit, and the walls and plants muffle the sounds of the city. A blindfolded visitor would hear the waterfall and the piping toads and not know the garden is in the city.

Year-round appeal

A garden can be interesting in all seasons if you grow the right plants. I follow three principles: keep the garden full; make sure there's always something in bloom; and grow a large variety of plants. Daffodils and tulips brighten the garden in spring and then give way to daylilies. The water lilies and lotuses flower in summer, along with many other plants that tolerate the heat, including cannas, roses, cleomes, daisies, daylilies, summer bulbs, trumpet vines, hibiscuses, ginger lilies, phloxes and oleanders. In the fall, the garden blooms with sedums, chrysanthemums, late roses, asters and helianthuses. The grasses have beautiful cotton-candy plumes, and the oak-leaf hydrangea turns a vivid red. For the last two years, I have allowed the grasses and other perennials to stand through the winter. Their dried stems and seedheads add interest to the winter garden.

Statues in unobtrusive niches await discovery. This bronze Buddha asks for alms beneath the trunks of a wax myrtle.

I garden for pleasure. Working in the garden is relaxation and comfort to the soul. When I come home from work, I turn on the lights outside before I turn on the lights in the house. I love to work among the plants at night; the colors change: the reds glow, and the greens and blues shine. The grey foliage of artemesia looks like icing on a cake. The marble statue of a shepherd gleams.

Gardening is a personal art, but I love to share my yard and plants. The most common question visitors ask is, "When do you have time to do all of this?" The answer is that there is not that much work, and I do a little every day. Having no lawn saves lots of time. The plants are nearly maintenance-free and so close together that there's little weeding. I also mulch everywhere with pine straw. If the garden were work, I wouldn't do it.

Visitors also ask how I know what plants to grow and where to put them. I'm not a trained gardener. I do what I want and what I think might look right. I mix colors as I please. Only twice have I made color combinations that I didn't like, and the remedy was simple: I moved the plants. The books recommend pinching chrysanthemums in spring and summer so they stay bushy and cover themselves with flowers in the fall. I don't pinch my chrysanthemums, and they flower once or twice in summer and again in fall. The point is to do what you like and enjoy it. You're the gardener. □

Walter Bull gardens in Columbia, South Carolina.

An allée of potted plants squeezes between the house and the property line. In what would otherwise be a barren stretch of masonry, the author grows a wide range of plants, among them camellias and azaleas on the right and a number of trees, including several standards, behind the wall on the left.

A Small World
Japanese-inspired garden evokes larger landscapes

by Monty Monsees

Visitors are usually surprised by the scope of the garden in my small front yard. In an area only 46 ft. by 42 ft. is a Japanese-inspired landscape of dwarf conifers and perennials, carefully placed stepping-stones and stone lanterns, and a dry pond. Along the edges of the property, rhododendrons and ferns grow in the shade of tall trees.

I must admit that when I look at photos I took when I moved here 25 years ago, I'm surprised, too. Carved out of a slope at the north end of the Berkeley Hills, my lot was a standard suburban rectangle, 6 ft. higher than my neighbor's site on one side, 6 ft. lower than the neighbor's on the other. The compacted, poorly draining clay soil was barren.

I soon replaced the top 6 in. of clay with sandy loam, and planted a lawn and some trees in the front yard and a Japanese-style garden in the rear. I'd never created a Japanese garden before, but I'd studied books about them and visited many. I liked their naturalistic look and harmonious feeling—they reminded me of a wooded countryside and of the western wilderness areas where I'd backpacked.

Everything grew well. The climate here, about ten miles from the Pacific Ocean, is one of California's best for gardening. Warmer, sunnier and less foggy than areas closer to the water, it's hot only occasionally and winter temperatures seldom drop to freezing.

Ten years later I became fascinated with rhododendrons, and I began collecting many rare, unusual or dwarf varieties, growing them mostly in containers. My fascination subsequently extended to dwarf conifers and low-growing ferns, and I accumulated a potted collection of these plants, too. The containers soon overran the backyard and the shady areas of my front lawn—the neighbors thought I had started a nursery.

Four years ago, having recently retired, I decided to begin a new front-yard garden with this abundant supply of plants. I wanted a peaceful garden that would keep me in touch with nature. I wanted it to be private, laid out so that each view from the house or garden would reveal new details. I wanted the garden to be inter-esting year round, and, finally, I wanted to plant out as much of my collection as possible without creating a crowded jumble.

Privacy wasn't much of a problem. Trees I had planted years before screened the yard from an adjacent house and the street. They would lend a perfect habitat for my rhododendrons. But I wondered what to do in the sunny areas closer to the house. I'm not sure what triggered the idea, but one day I decided to make another Japanese garden there, merged with the adjacent rhododendron plantings. The Japanese idea of a garden as a daily substitute for the natural landscape, reflecting its beauty and balance, suited me, and the Japanese are also masters at including many plants in a small space while making it appear unified and spacious.

I adopted design techniques from a number of different Japanese gardening styles, as the Japanese themselves had done centuries before with Chinese techniques, and I applied them to both the Japanese and rhododendron areas in the front yard. I tried to direct the viewer's eye: from low-growing plants near the house to tall ones framing the garden's perimeter, and from details within the garden to scenery beyond its borders. I

tried to direct the viewer's feet, too, so the garden would be explored from many perspectives, each one revealing surprises. I chose a few plant groups rather than many, and made use of the variety within each group. I paid close attention to scale, both within groupings and for the garden as a whole.

The rhododendron woodland

I began to lay out the garden in the fall of 1984, concentrating most of my efforts on the rhododendrons and the woodland area. I couldn't plant all my rhododendrons, so I selected 55 of my favorites and reluctantly gave the rest away. I picked varieties that are rare, fragrant or photogenic; those that have handsome foliage (rhododendron flowers last only about two weeks); and those that would, as a group, bloom from January to June. I laid out a slightly curving pathway leading through the trees. (I never put down a surface, but relied on footsteps to eventually wear one in.) Then I set out the containers of rhododendrons and arranged them until they looked good from different vantage points in the garden and the house. I avoided straight lines of sight—curves lead the eye on a longer journey, in-

Beginning in 1984, Monsees remade his conventional front yard (below), combining a Japanese area (above, foreground) with a woodland-like planting of rhododendrons. Inspired by Japanese landscape design, he artfully fit many plants in his small yard, creating a spacious- and natural-looking garden with year-round interest. To the right of the entrance sidewalk is a dry gravel pond and a fir-bark path leading to a water basin. Just beyond, two mounds planted with dwarf conifers are separated by a path to the rhododendron area. A Zen-style planting is just visible to the left of the sidewalk. A grouping of cream-flowered Pacific Coast irises (*Iris Douglasiana*), polished pebbles and mondo grass (facing page) highlights the area adjacent to the dry pond.

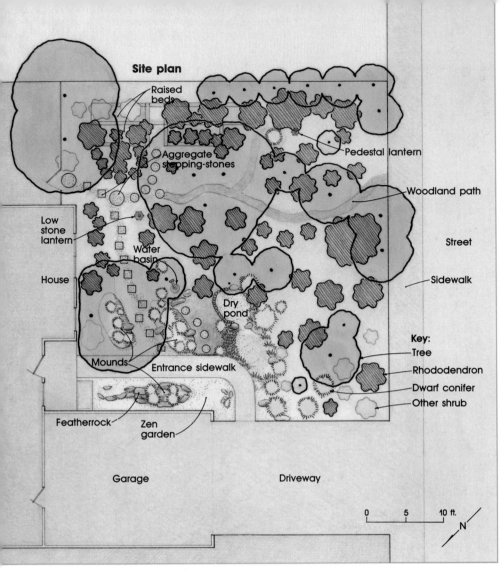

Site plan

Raised beds

Aggregate stepping-stones

Pedestal lantern

Low stone lantern

Water basin

Woodland path

House

Street

Dry pond

Sidewalk

Mounds

Entrance sidewalk

Key:
Tree
Rhododendron
Dwarf conifer
Other shrub

Featherrock

Zen garden

Garage

Driveway

0   5   10 ft.

N

creasing the feeling of space and revealing the garden's contents a little at a time.

Most of the rhododendrons are dwarf forms, growing no taller than 3 ft. in ten years; a few others range from 4 ft. to 7 ft. Planting in tiers of ascending height makes a garden seem larger, so I set the small rhododendrons toward the center of the yard and the taller ones closer to the property line, where they also help enclose the garden. Several of the taller varieties planted in two timber-framed raised beds in the eastern corner of the yard screen most of my neighbor's house from view.

Two stone lanterns add a human touch to the "forested wilderness" I've tried to evoke in the rhododendron area. A low one marks the beginning of the woodland path. It comes into view as you walk through the Japanese area. Then, when you reach the first lantern, a tall pedestal lantern can be seen deep within the rhododendron area. This lantern, framed by two birch trees, is also a distant focal point when seen from my bedroom window.

As you draw close to the lanterns, details of the plantings around them catch your eye. Around the low lantern, I planted small plants: a deer fern (*Blechnum*

Spicant), a hybrid marsh marigold and dwarf rhododendrons. Larger plants highlight the larger lantern. The fragrant white flowers of *Rhododendron cubittii* 'Ashcombe' drape over it in February. In November, when the rest of the garden is flowerless, the dwarf, pink-flowered *R. kiusianum* brightens the lantern. Just beyond the tall lantern, a Japanese cherry tree (*Prunus yedoensis* 'Akebono') adds its pink blossoms in the spring. These Japanese touches in the rhododendron area help unify the whole garden.

Each view of the rhododendron area reveals something slightly different. From the front of the house, I see a tableau, with the Japanese area in the foreground. Walking along the path within the shaded area, I'm surrounded by birches and rhododendrons and can only glimpse the Japanese garden. Through branches of the taller plants, I can see tall Monterey pines at the top of an embankment across the street. This borrowed scenery makes the garden seem bigger.

Rhododendrons are shallow-rooted and need soil that drains well—not a characteristic of my clay. So I planted them in mounds of handmade soil mix. For each mound, I used 15 gal. of com-

posted fir bark, 5 gal. of sandy loam, about 1 gal. of composted oak leaf mold, 1 gal. of horticulture-grade perlite and 1 cup of Shasta fertilizer formulated for acid-loving plants. To plant, I set each root ball on the ground and anchored any plant more than 1½ ft. tall with 1-in.-square redwood stakes to keep it from wobbling in my loose soil mix, driving the stakes flush against the sides of the root ball, at least 6 in. below its bottom and level with the soil surface. Then I mounded moistened soil mix around the root ball and tapered the mound to ground level, or connected it to a nearby mound, creating a larger mound or a low ridge. A thick layer of pine-needle mulch finished the job and hid the tops of the stakes. I've planted alpine strawberries between some of the rhododendrons, and I've scattered ferns and low-growing flowering plants throughout the shaded area.

The Japanese garden
My ideas for this area only gradually came into focus. I decided to emulate Japanese gardens of the 8th to 11th centuries, which were designed to suggest much larger spaces in nature—stones evoke hills or mountains, planted mounds suggest islands, dwarf conifers stand for large trees, and so on. The main features of my Japanese garden are a dry pond and two large mounds, which angle diagonally away from the entrance sidewalk; two slightly curved stepping-stone paths, which lead into the garden from the sidewalk; and a stone water basin, the main accent in the Japanese area. A Zen garden next to the garage is the last major element I installed.

From the start, I wanted a pond. But a real pond seemed too much trouble to install and maintain, so I decided to do what Japanese Zen Buddhists have done since the 15th century—use gravel to suggest water (see photo, pp. 84-85). The pond would be an important focal point, so I staked out its hourglass shape on a diagonal to the entrance sidewalk. A diagonal line of sight within a square area gives the impression of spaciousness by directing the eye down a longer path than a horizontal or vertical line would.

On one side, I buried a semicircle of 6-in.-long redwood logs on end to contain the gravel. A small beach of black pebbles between the logs and the sidewalk balances the composition. I leveled the pond bottom, laid thick black plastic to suppress weeds, slit holes in it for drainage and covered it 3 in. to 4 in. deep with coarse gravel. Sometimes I rake the gravel into wave-like patterns, but even without raking, it still gives the illusion of water as long as I clear away fallen leaves.

I grouped plants and rocks on each side of the pond. Each cluster contains an odd number of elements to suggest na-

A pine-needle-covered path meanders through the rhododendron woodland (above). A tall pedestal lantern, seen in the distance through the birch trees, draws a stroller's attention and composes the scene. A glimpse of scenery beyond the trees enlarges the vista of the garden. The pink flowers of an unnamed Whitney-cross rhododendron, blooming just beneath those of the rhododendron 'Sugar Pink', and the red flowers of 'Jim Drewry' brighten the April garden. In contrast to the less formal woodland, the Japanese area includes compositions such as this dwarf spruce draping over a mound of Scotch moss (below). Mondo grass tucked against a rock, and a dwarf Canadian hemlock in the background complete the arrangement.

ture's randomness, but I attempted to balance the groupings around the pond by using plants or rocks in similar positions on each side. The overall effect is a visual tension that draws the eye back and forth across the pond, and makes the viewer more aware of the details. For example, I made two small mounds across from one another near the center of the pond. A dwarf spruce (*Picea Abies* 'Pendula') and a dwarf Canadian hemlock (*Tsuga canadensis* 'Prostrata') on one side are balanced by a mini-dwarf mugo pine (*Pinus Mugo* var. *Mugo* 'Mitch') and a clump of mondo grass (*Ophiopogon japonicus*) on the other. A weathered featherrock (a gray, lightweight rock of solidified lava foam) juts out into the pond from each mound, forming a gateway through which the "water" flows. I wedged three round stones against the "upstream" side of one of these rocks, so it looked as if water had lodged them there.

At the upper end of the pond, I planted a tall Japanese maple (*Acer palmatum*) with particularly beautiful fall color. I also planted an evergreen dogwood (*Cornus capitata*) here as a focal point—it decorates the garden in May with white flowers, and in winter with red fruits that

hang like Christmas-tree ornaments.

The mounds near the sidewalk are each about 4 ft. wide by 8 ft. long, planted with dwarf conifers and ground covers. I built them like the rhododendron mounds: I set the root balls of the dwarf conifers on the ground and shaped my soil mix around each into an elongated oval with gradually sloping sides, about 1 ft. high. Then I planted the ground covers. I like the rounded form and horizontal growth of dwarf conifers, which seem to foster a restful, harmonious feeling, unlike the active, dynamic feeling I get from conifers with conical crowns and vertical lines.

I've nicknamed the mound nearest the pond the "Blue Mound" for the Colorado blue spruce (*Picea pungens glauca* 'R.H. Montgomery') that dominates it as well as for the other blue-green needled dwarf conifers planted there. I planted Scotch moss (*Sagina subulata* 'Aurea') as a ground cover on this mound. Green-needled dwarf conifers cover the mound near the house. This mound is carpeted with Irish moss (*S. subulata*), whose dull-green color doesn't call attention to itself. Neither ground cover is a true moss, and both grow slowly. It took two and a half years for the 2-in. squares I planted on 4-in. centers to fill in. I placed other small featherrock throughout the Japanese area, most of them partially buried in the mounds. They're easy to transport, and come in different sizes and shapes.

The longer path, stepping-stones set in coarse gray-white gravel, leads between the two mounds to the rhododendron area. The other path, of stepping-stones set in fir bark, leads past the pond to the water basin. I curved the paths so that people would walk slowly and notice details along the way. A wild, moss-like plant has naturalized in the gravel of the longer path, blending it with the adjacent mounds, while the contrasting color and texture of the fir bark direct attention to the basin.

A shallow ditch along the length of one side of the long path helps drain runoff from the yard. I dug the ditch 4 in. deep by 4 in. wide, filled it with pea-size gravel and laid down a 4-in. topping of the gravel over the whole path. Square and round stepping-stones (commercial, precast ones made of coarse aggregate concrete about 3 in. thick) rest on the gravel. To lay the fir-bark path, I spread heavy black plastic on the already compacted ground, laid the stepping-stones on the plastic and filled around them with 3 in. of medium-size bark chips.

Stone water basins are part of the Japanese tea ceremony. Traditionally they're placed close to the ground, so as guests crouch to wash their hands they feel humble. Although I didn't plan to host tea ceremonies, I liked the feeling of thankfulness and reverence associated with a basin, as well as the sound of water trickling

into it. My basin cost $60, complete with bamboo spout. It's 18 in. in diameter and made of concrete, with a lotus-blossom design. I set it on the ground, tipped slightly forward so that water will flow out of it over a sea of polished black pebbles. In front of the sea of pebbles, I placed a flat rock to stand on, along with a higher one on the right side and another on the left. A buried hose supplies water to the spout. A tall Japanese maple shelters the basin, and dwarf rhododendrons nearby blend with the rhododendrons farther back.

The area along the garage wall was my greatest problem, and after much thought I decided to plant a Zen-style garden there. This style, which emphasizes simplicity and symbolism, seemed suited for the entry to my house, a natural pausing place. I decided to build a single mound and surround it with gravel, like an island in the sea. The sidewalk then becomes a bridge across the "water" of the sea and the pond. The area between the garage and the sidewalk is only 4 ft. wide, so I positioned the mound parallel to the walk. On the mound and extending into the gravel sea, 13 featherrock at various angles capture shifting light and shadow patterns throughout the day. The rocks'

shapes evoke memories of mountains I've climbed or admired from afar.

I planted four dwarf spruce trees (*Picea Abies* 'Nidiformis' and 'Little Gem') and Scotch moss on the mound, and surrounded it with a greater area of gravel than the other mounds, giving it a more austere look. I especially like an isolated arrangement near the driveway of three rocks and a bonsai dwarf larch (*Larix* sp.) underplanted with Scotch moss. From the kitchen window, the tiny larch appears to be even more distant than it is.

Not everyone appreciates the subtlety of Japanese design. My mailman thought the gravel sea was a shortcut to the mailbox by the front door—a reasonable assumption for someone who doesn't know about Zen gardens. I soon tired of raking his footprints out of the gravel. Rather than stay at home or write him a letter asking him to use the sidewalk, I put up a row of low stakes to prevent him from cutting across the gravel, but he stepped higher. I added string and he took longer strides. I moved the bonsai larch and three rocks to their present location to block his path. He moved his shortcut to the other side. I added three signs on tall stakes: "Look at the gravel, don't walk on

The gravel-filled dry pond suggests water and provides a visual resting place (left). Gray featherrock, adjacent to several small mound plantings, define a passageway such as water might form. From the vantage point of the house (above), the eye moves from the newly planted Scotch moss and dwarf conifers on the "Blue Mound" (foreground) up to the rhododendrons and trees beyond. Behind a Colorado blue spruce, *Rhododendron campylogynum* var. *cremastum*, a white-flowered viburnum (*Viburnum plicatum* forma *tomentosum* 'Fujisanensis') and the pink rhododendron 'Roseann' bloom in late March. Just in front of the red-flowering rhododendron 'Halfdan Lem', the spreading dwarf spruce is paired with a mugo pine on the opposite shore.

The sound of water trickling into a stone basin lends a peaceful feeling to the garden (right). The contrasting foliage colors and textures of the yellow-green Scotch moss, the Colorado blue spruce 'R.H. Montgomery', the deep-green Japanese false cypress (*Chamaecyparis obtusa*) and Japanese tassel fern (*Polystichum setosum*), and the spiky mondo grass add variety with just a few types of plants.

The Zen-style garden, seen from the kitchen window (below), was laid out to suggest an island in a sea. The featherrock cast shifting patterns of light and shadow. A tiny larch and a grouping of rocks at the far end (the "Mailman Arrangement") create a sense of distance.

it." He stepped between them. Finally, one day I saw him backtrack to read the signs, and the next day he walked up the sidewalk. I took down the signs, the string and the stakes, and dubbed the corner planting the "Mailman Arrangement."

Maintaining the garden involves regular watering with an automated system, deadheading, some hand-weeding, fertilizing, mulching and a little insect control. Deadheading the rhododendrons (carefully removing the dead flowers without damaging the new buds) is necessary for a heavy bud set the following year. The varieties in my garden bloom from January to June, so I deadhead piecemeal over several months, but I rather enjoy keeping in touch with my plants this way. So far, I've rarely pruned anything.

I never tire of looking at or wandering through the garden. By combining my passion for rhododendrons with my love of nature and appreciation for Japanese gardens, I've created a special place that keeps me close to the beauty and serenity of nature. □

Monty Monsees gardens in San Pablo, California, and specializes in macrophotography of rhododendrons.

The Tale of a Garden

A serene landscape traces the journey of life

A Japanese maple in autumn orange graces a path of lichen-covered stones. The red footbridge leads to the scene of an imaginary wedding, with the wedding ring symbolized by a round, stone wheel. The wedding is a highlight in the story of one man's life, from birth to old age, as told by the turns and forks and landscaping along the winding, uphill path of the author's Japanese garden.

by Wallace H. Gray

Inspired by memories of childhood visits to a special garden, I've made my own Japanese garden on a rocky hillside. The garden tells a story, tracing a man's journey through life, symbolized by the path winding up the hill. Conifers and small, deciduous trees are set off by the grays of stepping stones, bedrock and a gravel path.

When I was eight, my parents, both keen gardeners, took me to see the Japanese Garden at Tully in County Kildare, Ireland. The garden, built between 1906 and 1910, was an inspiration to me even at that early age. I so loved the well-pruned, almost stunted trees and shrubs set amidst water and well-placed rocks that I persuaded my parents to make annual trips to Tully for several years. The revelations I experienced there have stayed with me to this day.

Years later, after my wife and I had moved to the house in Connecticut where she had grown up over many summers, all my memories of Tully came crowding back. As I looked out at the front lawn—a sloping meadow of rock outcroppings, wild apple trees and poison ivy—I realized that I had found the site for my own Japanese garden. It suddenly seemed an easy exercise to prune wild trees and shrubs into the shapes I wanted. I was already growing sedums, from the most dwarfed varieties to a stunted 'Autumn Joy' that I had dwarfed by planting it in a rock crevice and literally starving it. Surely trees could be treated the same way, I thought. I had also tried five or six varieties of sempervivums, the succulent-leaved rosettes that many gardeners call hen-and-chickens. Sempervivums like it hot and dry in summer and don't seem to mind the northwest wind in the winter. I hoped they could live among the stones and sparse soil of the garden I planned to make. I was right. They are still thriving in the garden today.

Getting ready for the garden

Early one spring 24 years ago, with my wife's help, I burned off the meadow (burning is now illegal) and started removing sod, poison ivy, honeysuckle bushes and trees—one at a time, by hand. I suppose most gardeners would have trucked amendments in to augment the thin soil, but I chose, instead, to remove the soil and expose the bedrock beneath it. I took pains to avoid scraping the rock as I worked to expose it. I dug until I could feel the bedrock, then switched to a rake until I could see the rock. I finished clearing with a brush and a trowel. The work took several summers to finish. Since the whole bank was then very exposed to the main road, the process was of enormous entertainment to passersby.

When I finished clearing, I had half an acre for the Japanese garden. It ran uphill from the road and was adjacent to the remaining bit of meadow. Today, the meadow is mowed about every other week so that the grass has a look slightly coarser than a lawn. The meadow contrasts strongly with the very rocky Japanese garden. Along the edge I planted spruces, white pines, flowering shadblows (*Amelanchier*) and crabapples to make a tranquil setting.

A rustic fence separates the garden and the meadow. Its design evolved mostly from trial and error, but it keeps the Oriental mood of the garden. (See photo on p. 88.) It is a type of wattle fence, but the maple saplings are wired, not woven. (Weaving would have been attractive too, but it requires that the saplings be wet so they'll be flexible, and the whole process would have taken more time than I could afford to spend.) The fence requires replacement every few years, and each new one gives the garden a completely different look.

Steps created the theme

A gravel and stone path that meanders from the bottom of the driveway up to the house is the backbone of the garden. I created the path and planted the garden in sections, moving up from the road. I collected flat stones from everywhere I visited, from the Adirondacks, Cape Cod and Montauk on Long Island, to the Cottswolds in Gloucestershire, England. After two or three years, I had enough stones and was ready to dig out the pathways. I dug, put down plastic sheeting, placed the stepping stones, and added gravel out to the width of the plastic. Stone edging holds the gravel in place. The garden was named at this stage by my daughter, who was then eight years old. She was so enchanted by the steps up the pathway that she called them "The Steps of Life."

Not all Japanese gardens tell stories, but mine does. As the path zigzags up the hill, it tells of a man's journey through life with all life's joys and tragedies. The main path is the journey; all entrances into life come from the left, and

Fallen crabapples glow against lichen-covered granite. The garden's venerable look lends it serenity.

As the path disappears uphill, late sun tints a sapling fence and the purple leaves of a small Japanese maple.

The garden's story

A tour of the garden starts at the "Cave of Birth" where the child takes his first steps of knowledge. The small cave, which I made of rocks, is now covered with climbing hydrangea *(Hydrangea anomala petiolaris)*. It sits on a circle of gravel across the driveway from the entrance to the Japanese garden. The first steps of knowledge cross the driveway into the garden, and at this stage the boy's parents leave the story. They sit on a stone bench beneath a crabapple tree and then make their way under an archway to happiness. I made this first archway myself, using small cedar logs to resemble a typical Japanese arch. It is not very high, but since it faces the fence and is at a dead end, no one needs to stoop because no visitor goes through it.

At first, the child travels on his own along a straight, narrow pathway. At the end, before the first turn, he looks into a dry pond, makes a wish and tosses a pebble into the "water" and watches the ripples. I make ripples daily with a rake in this dry sand pond. The young man kicks his heels up as the path turns and twists, but all the time he is climbing in knowledge.

The man then meets a woman who enters from the left. They go past a tranquil pond (of water) but, alas, have a quarrel and she leaves and follows a different pathway around a shrub, a Harry Lauder's walking stick *(Corylus avellana 'Contorta')*, which has marvelously twisted branches. After contemplation, she decides she loves him

Moss and a dwarfed white pine grow from pockets of soil in sloping granite. The outcropping of bedrock was originally covered with a thin layer of soil and a thicket of poison ivy. The author removed the soil and exposed the rock to create parts of his Japanese garden.

all permanent exits go off to the right. On the main path of the garden I used ⅜-in. washed gravel, but all other paths are of a finer washed gravel to define the different entrances and exits of the story. Lanterns light the way and mark life's milestones. There are small terra cotta lanterns that I bought in a garden shop, and larger ones made of concrete, which I antiqued with layers of stain and finished with a water-repellent sealer. I'm always keeping my eyes out for lanterns in my travels.

Garden-size bonsai

When the path first went in, all the trees were very small, and the stones and connecting rock outcroppings which made the beds were very obvious, so I overplanted. The idea was to soften the edges.

Because we couldn't afford large specimen trees, I experimented with small trees dug from fields and woods. My most successful efforts were with spruce, white pine, juniper and hemlock. I planted them in pockets between rocks and pruned them almost as one would prune a bonsai so they were the right scale for the area. Because they are pruned about once a year and are planted between rocks where their roots cannot take off, they remain dwarf. Many of these trees are still in the garden and have fooled collectors of miniature trees, who think they are natural dwarfs.

Another softening element in the garden is the growth of lichens on the rocks. It took about three years for the lichens to grow, so the change in the garden was a gradual one. I have seen friends, however, hasten the process by watering the rocks occasionally with about ½ pint of vinegar to a gallon of water.

after all and rejoins her young man for the journey of life.

Together, the young man and woman cross a small, red bridge and get married at the "Marriage Table." The bridge was made by a local carpenter from my design which had evolved through study of many Japanese gardens in books I have collected over the years. It is painted a bright red and, in order to ensure that no one crossing the bridge would slip, sand was mixed with the paint for the span. The marriage table is a large, flat, stone slab on stone supports. Next to it, I placed a small, antique sharpening stone in an upright position to suggest a wedding ring. The whole area is lighted by a special lantern.

Green rosettes of sempervivums, most smaller than a quarter, crowd together in the gravel beside a path.

mist cherry (*Prunus* 'Hally Jolivette') and a weeping cherry (*Prunus serotina pendula*) to a large rock elevated on two boulders to suggest a tomb: the end of their lives. The pathway curves by in tranquility, suggested by different sized stones.

Changes in the garden

Any garden, but particularly a Japanese garden, should change constantly, just as one changes objects inside a house. Every spring, I take out one or two trees or shrubs that aren't developing the way I'd like, and I add other new plants. This practice also opens up new vistas. I started the Japanese garden in 1968, and I don't suppose I shall ever finish it. Plants change, grow, obstruct and must be taken out. As I look back, I see that the garden might be considered a daunting undertaking. But it wasn't. It was a labor of love, and it remains a source of joy to my family and a place of serenity for me. ☐

Wallace H. Gray, who specializes in designing private gardens, lives in Washington, Connecticut.

The newly married couple continue on an upward climb from success to success and presently become the parents of two children. The children are represented by a narrow path of small stepping stones which enters from the left. Here there are some fine specimen trees: a horizontal silver spruce and a large weeping pine that I have pruned so visitors can look through the branches to views of other parts of the garden. I think the trees were in 2-gal. pots when I planted them, but over the years they have grown to stately size.

The family now reaches the "Peak of Success," a row of pointed rocks standing on end, with junipers (*Juniperus chinensis* 'Robusta') and false cypress (*Chamaecyparis obtusa* 'Filicoides') pruned into sharply pointed shapes. The man and woman sit on another stone bench to view their past and the mystery of life to come.

The pathway makes a steep turn and wanders down the hill again. Midway along the path there is a 40-to-50-year-old Chinese cork tree (*Phellodendron chinense*), which was the only tree of merit in the area when we moved here, planted by my father-in-law sometime in the 1940's. Here, the children leave to the right to find their own way past a wishing pool and through an arch. This arch is much bigger and more important than the one at the beginning of the garden. It was made of cedar and pressure-treated wood by a local carpenter using plans I drew, based on photos of an arch I admired. It stands about 5-ft. 9-in. high and is painted a greenish blue with white rubbed into the stain when it was still wet (see photo at right).

The man and woman continue on their path, which slopes gently down the hill, past another small pool, a

A weeping spruce cascades down a rocky slope. The stepping stones climb to an arch that invites visitors to pursue the next leg of the journey through the garden.

Red azaleas, white alyssum and green ferns cover the shady hillside above a flagstone patio. The author carved the patio from the hill and transformed the slope into a garden. (Photo taken at A on site plan, p. 92.)

Outdoor Room with View

A welcoming patio nestles into a hillside

by Patricia Dresel

Our backyard garden is an intimate extension of our home. My husband and I walk out the back door onto level flagstones to sit and enjoy brightly planted containers at the foot of a verdant hillside of ivy, azaleas and ferns. From indoors, we look out to the patio and hillside from every window along the back of the house. To transform our steep backyard into a garden room, we cut into the hill to increase a level area beside the house. We held the slope at bay with a series of curving stone walls. We paved the patio with stones, carved steps up the hill and planted a backdrop of ornamental plants. You, too, can transform a troublesome slope or make a patio into a bouquet of color if you follow the same design principles we did.

The double trunk of an old live oak rises from a patio of flat stones and pebbly concrete. The rock retaining wall in the background helps make the patio an extension of the house. (Photo taken at B on site plan.)

Designing the garden

When we bought our property 30 years ago, it came with an uninspired cement patio ending at a steep, overgrown hillside. The fence that surrounded it held back tangled toyon bushes (*Heteromeles*) and poison oak.

We bought the property for several reasons. First, it had an endearing old double-trunked California live oak tree (*Quercus agrifolia*), other old oaks and several large bays (*Umbellularia californica*) scattered about the one-third-acre, pie-shaped lot. I loved the privacy of the backyard, which was nestled into a hillside. And lastly, Marin County, California, was beautiful, glorying in a damp, green January. Here I thought I could make my dream garden.

Reclaiming the hillside

We immediately set to clearing the hillside and planting a garden on its steep slope. The first thing we needed was access, so we designed and installed a stairway. This rustic union of railroad ties and washed stones winds its way up the hill and through the trees. Its sweeping curve was so graceful that we decided to incorporate curves wherever we could as we designed the rest of our garden and patio. (See site plan on p. 92.)

Next we pruned oaks and toyon. We cleared broom and poison oak. Then we planted a ground cover of prostrate *Pyracantha* 'Santa Cruz' for low maintenance as well as beauty. We added flowers and shrubs here and there, and the more of ourselves we put into the garden, the more we loved it.

An intimate patio

Seventeen years later, we found the money and time to enlarge the patio. We hired a landscape architect to help with the design. Contractors broke up the old slab and dug into the hill, enlarging the patio floor into a footprint shape 65 ft. long by 20 ft. wide. The instep is only 10 ft. wide.

We surfaced the new patio with flagstones set in pebbly concrete. The flags are subtle shades of gray, blue or green and are set in a random pattern. The patio has the informal look that I had imagined nearly 17 years earlier. And it's a good thing that we entertain casually, because the patio's greatest asset is also its only drawback—the uneven surface is hard to walk on in high heels.

We built the new retaining wall with rock gardening in mind. It's natural-looking, with plenty of dry-laid fieldstone niches for plants. The wall incorporates a short section, built by a previous owner, which was functional but not gracefully designed. We added new sections to each end of the original wall, creating a finished wall that stretches from one side of the property to the other in one lovely, sinuous curve.

The retaining wall varies in height. The midsection ranges from about 3 ft. tall to 5 ft. tall. From the center it slopes gradually, tapering to one row of rocks at each end.

Construction was complicated by the problem of how to preserve my favorite oak tree. I knew that oaks don't take kindly to having their roots disturbed, and I feared that extending the new patio floor over the earth where this one grew would reduce oxygen and moisture at its roots. So we drilled small holes through the concrete in concentric circles from the trunk to the drip line. A tree service applies fertilizer through the holes in spring. The tree adjusted and after 12 years still thrives.

The new patio needed drainage. Because our property is at the foot of a steep hill, it floods during winter rain storms. The contractors dug a ditch at the base of the hillside, laid in drain pipes and connected them to our storm sewers. They also built a slight hump into the patio so that water flows toward the drain pipes along the retaining wall and toward the open ends of the patio.

We also installed catch basins where the rock wall meets the patio. Lined with concrete, the basins are 10 in. in diameter and 4 in. deep, with drain pipes at the bottom that connect them to the storm sewers. A clever trick disguises them. While the concrete was wet, the builders recessed a metal grate in each basin, pressed a stone into the wet concrete and then removed it until the concrete dried. Each stone fits its basin like a puzzle piece, blending into the pattern of the patio. When storms come, we lift the stones and put the catch basins to work.

Subtle lighting lets us enjoy the patio in the evening. The contractor installed conduit and wiring before he laid the surface. Then he tucked small light fixtures into the rock retaining wall and along the hillside stairs and installed spotlights to illuminate the larger trees and the hillside garden.

For the finishing touch to the patio we designed a curved, redwood bench that fits against the rock wall. In addition to providing seating, the bench breaks up the expanse of rock wall and hides an eyesore—stains caused by mud that oozes down the hillside and onto the patio during winter rains. It directs attention instead to a nearby collection of colorful container plants.

A sweep of color

Content at last with my patio and rock wall, I happily began planting. First I laid a foundation of evergreen plants—azaleas and ferns in shady areas and junipers and rosemary in sunny areas and filtered shade. I planted ivy to soften the relentless gray of the rocks. A friend handed me a bag of hen-and-chickens (*Echeveria*), and I tucked them into every crevice I could find. Their little rosettes have multiplied and traveled between the rocks, filling the cracks in a delightful way. I also added a variety of sedums—I love the way they bunch up and tumble over the ledges.

Where the hillside meets the top of the wall I planted perennials—coreopsis, Stokes' aster (*Stokesia*), black-eyed Susans, pink 'Clara Curtis' daisies and fringed blue asters. Behind them I planted Spanish lavender (*Lavandula*

stoechas) and white-flowered chrysanthemums. Higher up the hill, dividing the flowers from the pyracantha, are delphiniums and pink coneflowers. All except the delphiniums are drought-tolerant—an important consideration in this part of California, which is suffering rainfall shortages.

There are some annuals that I can't do without, including lobelias (the more the merrier), violas and pansies—who could survive a season without their cheery faces? Impatiens provides color in the darkest corners of the patio. Sometimes I put in batches of marigolds and other times I count on volunteers. Blue forget-me-nots thrive singularly and in drifts. Sweet alyssum, sturdy and aggressive, seeds itself in every conceivable niche, spilling over the rocks like foam.

When the annuals are working in concert with the perennials, I stand in my dining room, squint one eye and think about what is needed to make the picture perfect. If it is a splash of red (or yellow or blue...), off I go to the nearest nursery for whatever it is to make my color scheme right.

Container color— Containers of flowering plants add color and sculptural interest to the patio. I think planting containers is like making a bouquet. You combine plants of different heights, different shapes and different colors. I always place cascading plants at the edges to spill over the rims of the containers. My favorites include violas, lobelias, alyssums, petunias and the tiny, gold-flowered daisy *Dyssodia tenuiloba*.

White flowers intensify vibrant colors in daylight, and they stand out in twilight and under electric lights. My favorite spring whites are candytuft (*Iberis*), white tulips and white fairy primrose (*Primula malacoides*). In summer I rely on marguerites, petunias and mounds of miniature dianthus. One of my most effective containers has white geraniums underplanted with white lobelias.

Site plan

Toyons

Azaleas

Rock wall

C

D

B

Original patio

House

Photos taken from lettered positions

N

Oaks

Railroad tie steps

Rock wall

Bench

A

Double trunk oak

Illustration: Vince Babak

I think a patio should have one or two unique containers. One of mine is shaped like a large, white tortoise. It looks smashing filled with red geraniums. Our son brought an even bigger ceramic turtle home from Mexico. Selecting plants for the turtles is one of my favorite spring projects.

Because containers are portable, I can extend their growing season by placing them where conditions best suit the plants. To prolong the life of sun-sensitive plants like violas, I move them out of the blistering midday sun and put them in the shade. Then back they go when the sun goes down. If I can't water for a day or two, I put the containers in the shade where they'll stay moist until I get home.

Color through the seasons

Our garden provides beauty throughout the year. In March the azaleas are blazing mounds of magenta, pink and white. The baby's-tears and ferns in the shady areas are lush and green. I plant primulas of all varieties. Though they're perennials, I treat them as annuals, plugging them in wherever I want low, bright color. I indulge in new bulbs every year (our winters are too warm to establish them). I can hardly wait for the display of irises, tulips and daffodils. Violas and Iceland poppies, planted in late February, come out in late March along with crisp, white iberis.

I think the garden is at its colorful best in summer when the patio is brimming with my container-bouquets of annuals.

Winter is less colorful, but the trees and shrubs take on new vitality in the rejuvenating winter rains. The shady part of the hillside directly beneath the oak tree has two very large toyon bushes that are filled with clusters of bright red berries, and the pyracantha on the hill is also a cheery red and green. My husband's favorite view of our patio and hillside garden is from his seat in the dining room on a rainy winter evening when the leaves of the shrubs, ferns and bergenia gleam wetly in the glow of the outdoor lights.

What a long way our garden has come in 30 years! The hillside has filled in. The old oaks continue to spread their umbrellas over us. And we're still here, our roots planted as firmly as the oaks'. ∎

Patricia Dresel gardens in Greenbrae, California.

White alyssum and _Chrysanthemum paludosum_ daisies bloom in cool contrast to magenta schizanthus and orange and yellow nemesia. The colorful display is rooted along the top of a rock retaining wall. (Photo taken at C on site plan.)

Steps made from railroad ties and tamped gravel climb the hillside above the author's patio. Clay pots ornament the corners of the steps. (Photo taken at D on site plan.)

Index

A

Anti-dessicants, winter-proofing with, 46
Arbors:
    over front walk, 18
    of pleached pears, 46
    See also Trellises.

B

Brink, Joan, on Pacific Northwest cottage
    garden, 24-28
Bull, Walter, on crowded city lot, 76-79

C

California:
    front-yard garden in, 14-17
    hillside garden in, 90-93
    Japanese-inspired garden in, 80-85
    mature hillside garden in, 29-33
    small hillside garden in, 48-51
    suburban garden in, 72-75
Chaparral, plants of, 30, 32
Colorado, Rocky Mountain garden for,
    52-56
Containers:
    for hillside patio, 92-93
    in city garden, 78
    in suburban garden, 75
Cottage gardens:
    designing, 18-23, 64
    plants for, 64-67
Courtyard, back-garden, 26-28

D

Davidson, Sylvia, garden of, 48-51
Dresel, Patricia, on California hillside
    garden, 90-93

E

Edgings, of wooden shingles, 13
Entryway, plants for, 16-17
Estabrook, F. Reed, Jr., on 40-year
    garden, 8-13

F

Fences, framing garden with, 26, 27
Ferns:
    favorites for shady garden in Louisiana,
      62
    sources for, 62
Fountains, for formal gardens, 46-47
Fragrance, and garden design, 28
Front yard. *See* Entryway.

G

Gainey, Ryan, romantic cottage garden
    of, 18-23
Garden design:
    curbside landscape, 68-71
    foliage in, 46
    formal, 42-47
    formal suburban, 72-75
    Japanese-inspired, 80-85
    limited space, for, 14-17
    principles of, 42-46
    shady passageway, 34-36
    small yard and entry, 14-17
    for telling a story, 86-89
    urban, 24-28, 76-79
    wooded, 58-63
    See also types of gardens.
Georgia, romantic cottage garden in,
    18-23
Geraniums, hardy, in coastal Oregon
    garden, 39
Goddard, Ragna Tischler, on formal
    gardens, 42-47
Gray, Wallace H., on Japanese garden,
    86-89
Ground covers:
    for garden slope, 10
    for pond border, 12, 13
    for shade, 46
    for sun, 46

H

Hansen, Constance, on plant collector's
    garden, 37-41
Haskell, Ruth Rohde, on Ryan Gainey's
    garden, 18-23
Hedges, miniature, plants for, 46
Herb gardens, formal, 42-47
Hillside gardens:
    heavily planted, urban, 48-51
    mature, natural, 29-33
    with patio, 90-93

I

Iris, mixed 40s, description, 39, 41
Irrigation, system for, 10

J

Japanese gardens:
    as inspiration for garden design, 80-85
    for telling a story, 86-89

K

Kane, Mark, on small hillside garden,
    48-51
Knot gardens:
    designing, 45, 46
    plants for, 46

L

Landscaping. *See* Garden design.
Lawns:
    in dry mountain climate, 55, 57
    making, 9
Licht, Avis Rappoport, on designing small
    front yard with entry, 14-17
Louisiana, wooded garden in, 58-63

M

Mannion, Tom, on curbside landscape,
    68-71
Menard, Alice, garden of, 72-75
Miller, Hortense, on mature California
    garden, 29-33
Monsees, Monty, on small Japanese
    garden, 80-85

The 18 articles in this book originally appeared in *Fine Gardening* magazine.
The date of first publication, issue number and page numbers for each article are given below.

If you enjoyed this book, you're going to love our magazine.

A year's subscription to *Fine Gardening* brings you the kind of hands-on information you found in this book, and much more. In issue after issue—six times a year—you'll find articles on nurturing specific plants, landscape design, fundamentals and building structures. Expert gardeners will share their knowledge and techniques with you. They will show you how to apply their knowledge in your own backyard. Filled with detailed illustrations and full-color photographs, *Fine Gardening* will inspire you to create and realize your dream garden!

To subscribe, just fill out one of the attached subscription cards or call us at 1-203-426-8171. And as always, your satisfaction is guaranteed, or we'll give you your money back.

Taunton
BOOKS & VIDEOS
for fellow enthusiasts

The Taunton Press 63 S. Main Street, P.O. Box 5506, Newtown, CT 06470-5506